UNIVERSITY OF NORTH CAROLINA AT CHAPEL HILL
DEPARTMENT OF ROMANCE LANGUAGES

NORTH CAROLINA STUDIES
IN THE ROMANCE LANGUAGES AND LITERATURES

Founder: URBAN TIGNER HOLMES

Distributed by:

UNIVERSITY OF NORTH CAROLINA PRESS
CHAPEL HILL
North Carolina 27514
U.S.A.

NORTH CAROLINA STUDIES IN THE
ROMANCE LANGUAGES AND LITERATURES
Number 190

CLOWN AT THE ALTAR:
THE RELIGIOUS POETRY OF MAX JACOB

CLOWN AT THE ALTAR:
THE RELIGIOUS POETRY OF MAX JACOB

BY

JUDITH MORGANROTH SCHNEIDER

CHAPEL HILL

NORTH CAROLINA STUDIES IN THE ROMANCE
LANGUAGES AND LITERATURES
U.N.C. DEPARTMENT OF ROMANCE LANGUAGES

1978

Library of Congress Cataloging in Publication Data

Schneider, Judith Morganroth.
  Clown at the altar.

  (North Carolina studies in the Romance languages and literatures; 190)
  Bibliography: p.
  1. Jacob, Max, 1876-1944 — Poetic works. I. Title. II. Series.

PQ2619.A17Z84   841'.9'12   78-236
ISBN 0-8078-9190-8

I.S.B.N. 0-8078-9190-8

DEPÓSITO LEGAL: V. 668 - 1978   I.S.B.N. 84-399-8122-8
ARTES GRÁFICAS SOLER, S. A. - JÁVEA, 28 - VALENCIA (8) - 1978

To Martin

CONTENTS

	Page
Preface	13
Introduction	19
I. METAPHYSICS: THEOSOPHY AND FAITH	29
II. POETIC THEORIES AND MYSTICISM	45
III. THE EVOLUTION AND THE DIALECTIC OF POETIC STYLE	67
IV. DIALOGISM	95
Conclusions	115
Appendix: Max Jacob and the Surrealists	123
Selected Bibliography	129

A LIST OF INITIALS AND EDITIONS USED
IN REFERENCES TO WORKS BY MAX JACOB

AP　　　　*Art poétique.* Paris: Emile-Paul Frères, 1922.

B　　　　*Ballades,* suivi de *Visions infernales, Fond de l'eau, Sacrifice impérial, Rivage, Les Pénitents en maillots roses.* Paris: Gallimard, 1970. Reissue of six earlier works.

CD　　　　*Le Cornet à dés.* Paris: Gallimard, 1945.

CJP　　　　*Conseils à un jeune poète.* Paris: Gallimard, 1945.

DP　　　　*Derniers poèmes en vers et en prose.* Paris: Gallimard, 1961.

DT　　　　*La Défense de Tartufe, extases, remords, visions, prières, poèmes, et méditations, d'un juif converti.* Introduction and notes by André Blanchet. Paris: Gallimard, 1964.

HC　　　　*L'Homme de cristal.* Paris: Gallimard, 1947.

LC　　　　*Le Laboratoire central.* Paris: Gallimard, 1960.

OBM　　　*Les Œuvres burlesques et mystiques de Frère Matorel, mort au couvent.* Paris: Kahnweiler, 1912.

SM　　　　*Saint Matorel.* Paris: Kahnweiler, 1911.

SM/OBM　*Saint Matorel,* suivi des *Œuvres burlesques et mystiques de Frère Matorel mort au couvent et du Siège de Jérusalem.* Paris: Gallimard, 1936.

PREFACE

Since Max Jacob's death in 1944 in the concentration camp of Drancy, as if under the sign of his martyrdom, critics have urged that the poet be taken more seriously. André Brissaud began his preface to the first volume of Jacob's *Correspondance* (1953) with the now familiar but still provocative question: "Le temps est-il venu de prendre Max Jacob au sérieux?" (p. I) As far as Brissaud was concerned, the moment of recognition had arrived, and, as evidence of the fact, he pointed to the cult of admiration that had arisen from the commemoration of the writer's death. Brissaud, nonetheless, warned of pitfalls inherent in commentary intended to edify a legend. Quite understandably, the first phase of Jacobian criticism had exhibited just that inclination. Five books published between 1944 and 1946 were rich in personal recollections and anecdotes, tended toward sentimentality if not idolatry, and discussed Jacob's writings only superficially.[1]

Thirty years after Drancy, we observe a logical evolution in the critical perspective. In 1971, Gerald Kamber in the preface to his *Max Jacob and the Poetics of Cubism* addressed himself "to specialists in contemporary French literature who have long lived with a serious gap in Jacob criticism."[2] A few years later, this gap seems nearly closed. From 1967 to 1973, six doctoral dissertations on Max Jacob were defended in France and the United States.[3] These studies, as well as several articles and books, have carefully examined

---

[1] See, Belaval, Billy, Lagarde, Parturier, Rousselot in my Selected Bibliography.
[2] (Baltimore and London: The Johns Hopkins Press, 1971), p. viii.
[3] See, Lévy, Pelletier, Plantier, St. Thomas, Schneider, Thau, in my Selected Bibliography.

aspects of his poetry, fiction, and writings on aesthetics. Kamber's book demonstrated analogies between Jacob's poetic method and cubism as well as his Baudelairian sources. Meanwhile, René Plantier published his *Max Jacob* (1972), the first extensive presentation of the religious themes in his writings. Still more recently, Una Pfau's *Zur antinomie der bürgerlichen satire* (1975) investigated Jacob's ironic critique of the bourgeoisie, while Annette Thau's *Poetry and Antipoetry* (1976) analyzed selected stylistic features. The second phase of Jacobian criticism has been facilitated by Gallimard's 1970 reedition, under the title *Ballades,* of six collections of poetry until then out of print and difficult to obtain. Continuing interest in his works is illustrated by the current Max Jacob series of *La Revue des Lettres Modernes,* edited by Jean de Palacio, and by the publication of the *Max Jacob Centennial* (1876-1976), a special number of *Folio* (Oct. 1976).[4]

My own contribution belongs to this second phase of Jacobian studies. Like most of Jacob's admirers, I was attracted first by the *Cornet à dés* and, then, by his writings on poetry. I wondered how his practice of poetry related to his poetic theories. Did they constitute a coherent system? Did they evolve coordinately? These inquiries finally led me to the conclusion that Jacob's theoretical writings were unsystematic, that they incorporated a spectrum of cubist and mystical views, often contradictory.[5] Such a poetics could not have served as a practical guide to poetic execution. And yet, Jacob's metaphysics, poetic theories, and poetry appeared to me connected through common stylistic processes and patterns of thought. The present monograph represents my endeavor to explore these correspondences.

In the meantime, I had become interested in Jacob's lyrical poetry of religious inspiration, published in collections subsequent to the *Défense de Tartufe* (1919): *Visions infernales* (1924), *Les Pénitents en maillots roses* (1925), *Fond de l'eau* (1927), *Sacrifice impérial* (1929), *Rivages* (1934), *Derniers poèmes en vers et en*

---

[4] The first issue of the Max Jacob series, RLM, Nos. 336-339 (1973), dealt with his prose poems; the second, RLM, Nos. 474-478 (1976), focused on his novels. Articles in these special numbers and in *Folio,* No. 9, are listed separately in my Selected Bibliography.

[5] See, J. M. Schneider, "Max Jacob on Poetry," MLR, 69 (Apr. 1974), 290-96.

prose (1945, posthumous), *L'Homme de cristal* (1948, posthumous). Although these volumes constitute more than half of Jacob's poetic production, they remain among the most ignored of his writings. Moreover, they have been subject to unsubstantiated judgments. For example, it is often supposed that Jacob's later poetry, as a result of his conversion to the Catholic faith, evolved toward a personal lyricism artistically less valid than the "objective" prose poems of the *Cornet*. This hypothesis may have been instigated by Jacob's own myth of the religious poet as a Lamartinian sentimentalist. Yet the assumption was probably reinforced by the aesthetic code of the Surrealists, dominating French poetry in the twenties and thirties. Before 1920, Aragon, Breton, and Soupault were associated with literary reviews on which Jacob also collaborated. Even so, as early as 1918, Breton and Aragon had included Jacob's name — accompanied by the epithets "God et famille" — in a list of traditionalist defenders of the outmoded notions of the "œuvre d'art" and "littérature."[6] Breton's manifestoes of surrealism subsequently omitted any mention of Max Jacob, although contemporary critics attribute a precursory influence to his *Cornet à dés*.[7] For the Surrealists, religious poetry was likely to be bad poetry.

Admittedly, one motive of this study was to establish the value of Jacob's later works. By illustrating the inventive character of his metaphysical beliefs (Ch. i), I hoped to demonstrate the compatibility of his religious vision and his poetic imagination. The conflict of occultism and orthodoxy in his texts on religion had its parallel in his poetics. And these oppositions accounted for Jacob's divergent views on the relation of poetry and faith. (Ch. ii) My discussion of his poetry indicates correspondences between contrasts

---

[6] Cf. Sylvia Kantariz, "Dada and the Preparations for Surrealism," *Australian Journal of French Studies*, 8, No. 1 (1971), 44-61. The list appeared in a manifesto, entitled "Treize études," published by Aragon and Breton in *SIC*, No. 29 (mai 1918), 3. For additional comments on Jacob's relations with the Surrealists, see, my Appendix, also, Tatiana Greene, "Max Jacob et le surréalisme," *French Forum*, 1 (Sept. 1976), 251-67.

[7] Cf. Wallace Fowlie, *Climate of Violence* (New York: Macmillan, 1967), p. 199: "In a lecture given at *Le Salon des Indépendants* in 1907, Apollinaire called attention to his friend Max Jacob. This was the first public acknowledgment of Jacob's work, but he had already for some time been composing poetry in accordance with principles that would eventually be taken over by the surrealists."

in style (Ch. iii), the dialogism of his rhetoric (Ch. iv), and the antitheses of his metaphysical and poetic theories. In Chapter iii, I approach his poetic style diachronically through an analysis of modifications resulting from Jacob's spiritual evolution. Throughout my commentary, I have focused on the complexity of form and theme that distinguishes his poems from embellished prayers. Adopting a structural method, I have insisted less on content and symbolic meaning, than on the pattern of duality underlying the semantic and formal elements of Jacob's writings.

In studying a fascinating poet, over a long period of time, I received assistance from talented scholars, whom I wish to thank in this preface. My interest in Max Jacob was initiated by Leroy C. Breunig at Barnard College and reinforced by Wallace Fowlie at Duke University. I was encouraged by discussions with the French poets Marcel Béalu and Jean Follain, members of the Société des Amis de Max Jacob. M. Didier Gompel, a cousin of the poet and collector of his manuscripts, rare editions, and paintings, kindly opened his collection to me. In my examination of the indispensable manuscripts of the Jacques Doucet Collection, I was assisted by M. François Chapon and Mlle. Cécile Jasinski, librarians; at the Bibliothèque Municipale of Quimper, by M. Sebastien Coïc. I was granted access to the Marguerite Mespoulet collection in the libraries of Columbia University through the offices of Professor Breunig. Without this generous help, I could not have accomplished my project.

Rochester, New York
June, 1977

Heureux celui qui d'un seul mot
Sut dire ton art et sa flamme,
Te saluant d'un nom si beau
Max le Jongleur de Notre-Dame!

    René Villard, *Aguedal* (1939)

  Il y avait un moment amer où l'on dit à Max Jacob: "Vous étiez poète?" Max a répondu: "Oui, quand même, moi j'étais poète." C'était sa modestie qui l'empêchait de dire poète dans le passé, le présent et l'avenir.

    Gertrude Stein, *Aguedal* (1939)

INTRODUCTION

"Rien ne me préparait au coup de foudre qui brûla d'un coup mon passé en septembre 1909 et fit naître en moi un homme nouveau," declared Max Jacob, while recounting for the last time the events of his religious conversion.[1] The thunderbolt which had nullified his past and given birth to a new man was the apparition of a "Corps Céleste" on the wall of his room at number 7, rue Ravignan, on Montmartre. (DT, p. 101)[2] An emanation of wonder and ecstasy amidst the homeliest surroundings marked the poet's evocations of his mystical vision. Dictated in 1939, his final account of the revelation recreated the atmosphere and emotion characteristic of earlier narrations:

> Après une journée de paisible travail à la Bibliothèque Nationale, rue Richelieu à Paris, je rentrais chez moi, ma grosse serviette de maroquin pleine de notes et de manuscrits. J'étais habillé comme on l'était à cette époque, j'avais un chapeau haut de forme et une redingote. Comme il faisait très chaud, je me réjouissais à l'idée de me mettre à mon aise. Après avoir enlevé mon chapeau, je m'apprêtais, en bon bourgeois, à mettre mes pantoufles quand je poussai un cri. Il y avait sur mon mur un Hôte. Je tombai à genoux, mes yeux s'emplirent de larmes soudaines. Un ineffable bien-être descendit sur moi, je restai immobile, sans comprendre. En une minute, je vivais un siècle. Il

---

[1] Jacob's "Récit de ma conversion" was originally published in 1951 in *La Vie intellectuelle*. My citation is from p. 290 of the version reprinted in Blanchet's Appendix to the edition of *La Défense de Tartufe* listed above.

[2] The expression "Corps Céleste" left the identity of the divine figure deliberately ambiguous. Jacob knew that Catholic dogma did not allow visions of God or his Son (DT, p. 293); and yet, he provided a complicated rationalization to support the conclusion: "C'est donc Dieu que j'ai vu." (DT, p. 158)

> me semble que tout m'était révélé. J'eus instantanément la notion que je n'avais jamais été qu'un animal, que je devenais un homme. Un animal timide. Un homme libre. Instantanément aussi, dès que mes yeux eurent rencontré l'Etre Ineffable, je me sentis déshabillé de ma chair humaine, et deux mots seulement m'emplissaient: *mourir, naître*. (DT, p. 290)

When Jacob indicated his unpreparedness for revelation, he was thinking of his rationalistic upbringing. He was born on July 12, 1876, in Quimper, Brittany, where his grandfather, an Alsatian Jew, had settled early in the nineteenth century. According to Jacob, after the death of his grandparents, there was no mention of God or religion in his home. His parents, whom he depicted as "israélites et voltairiens," taught him the principles of natural morality, but they valued, above all, knowledge, honors, titles, and material success. Jacob recounted that his schooling, too, was secular and provided him with no religious foundation. Yet he admitted that one element of his childhood, at least, exposed him to the Christian spirit. This was the religious life centered around the cathedral of Quimper. Jacob recalled with nostalgia the Holy Day processions made colorful by scattered flowers and traditional Breton costumes. He confessed, moreover, his envy of the participants, especially of his friends dressed in their communion clothes. His sense of exclusion from the ceremonies of the church fostered an apprehension of their mysteriously sacred essence. (DT, p. 289)

The religious fervor of Brittany, however, did not directly precipitate Jacob's conversion to the Catholic faith. For several years before the apparition of the *Corps Céleste,* Jacob had been living in Paris, where he was a familiar Bohemian figure (astrologist, mimic, impromptu singer, dancer, musician, and active homosexual) in the group of cubist painters and poets. When he spoke to his friends of his vision and religious sentiments, they responded with cynical quips. It was all the more difficult for Jacob's contemporaries to take his conversion seriously, since he led as derelict a life as ever, except for regularly attending confession at Sacré-Cœur. Just after his revelation, Jacob went to a local priest and asked to be baptized; when the request was refused, he did not renew it until five years later. In the meantime, he tried to interpret his vision through the science of symbolism, studied in the books of the kabbala at the Bibliothèque Nationale. To reinforce his Christian faith, he read St. Francis de Sales's *Introduction à la vie dévote,* the manual which became his guide to devotional meditation. Finally, in 1914, under the direction of Father Schaffner of the convent of Sion, Jacob began official preparations for his conversion. In February of 1915, the thirty-nine year old poet was baptized Cyprien Max Jacob, with his friend, Pablo Picasso, acting as godfather.

Shortly before baptism, Jacob had become discouraged because of delays in his religious instruction, which he considered fatally prolonged. But a second vision restored his hope. This time a haloed figure, protectively enveloping in his cape the children of Jacob's *concierge,* appeared on the screen of a movie theater, during the projection of a cloak-and-dagger film. "Le Christ au cinématographe," a poem inspired by the incident, exhibits Jacob's awareness of the dubious aspect of his faith. The poetic speaker, who invokes God as a witness to the truth of his apparitions, is interrupted by a skeptical query from his confessor. His reply to the priest combines religious fervor and parodic humor. For while his allusion to the Lord's power of working miracles suggests intense mysticism, his flippant wit creates an ironic undertone:

> Donc, la première fois, Tu vins dans ma maison.
> Et la seconde fois, au Cinématographe . . .
> "Vous allez donc alors au Cinématographe,
> Me dit un confesseur, la mine confondue.
> —Eh! mon père! le Seigneur n'y est-il pas venu?"
>
> (DT, pp. 128-29)

The coveted baptism was itself a cause of disillusionment. Jacob noted in the *Défense de Tartufe,* his spiritual autobiography, his expectations not of salvation, but of a moral revolution. In this hope, he had been disappointed. (p. 163) In effect, no obvious change in his life-style occurred during the years immediately following his baptism, referred to in the *Défense* as the time of "La décadence ou mystique et pécheur." In confessions relating to the period, Jacob accused himself of denigrating his religion for the sake of amusing friends and of destroying friendships through calumny and impure intentions. Nevertheless, the moral transformation he had desired became a fact of his existence in 1921, when he moved from Paris to Saint-Benoît-sur-Loire, a small town south of Orléans, with a romanesque cathedral and a history as a monastic center. There Jacob remained for six years in quiet retreat; he followed the Divine Services assiduously and wrote poems, novels, meditations, and letters to numerous correspondents. Although there were occasional visits from Parisian friends, his correspondence indicates that he associated spiritual peace with resignation to solitude: "Il me reste le chagrin de ne plus voir quelques chers amis et de ne plus rencontrer certaines physionomies ou sympathiques ou respectables. Tout se paie, même le bonheur... surtout le bonheur et j'achète le mien au prix de grands sacrifices sur l'autel de l'amitié. J'y gagne aussi de connaître l'humanité vraie, celle qu'à Paris les potins et l'esprit décorcachent sans cesse." [3] For Jacob, Saint Benoît and Paris symbolized moral antipodes.

If the new man in Jacob was born instantly in a fortuitous thunderclap, his survival demanded a continuous enterprise marked by persistent conflicts. No longer able to resign himself to provincial isolation, Jacob returned to Paris, where, from 1927 to 1936, he led an existence later described as "la plus criminelle de ma vie." [4] Although Jacob numbered homosexuality among his most detested "crimes," he usually referred to it in abstract terms, as in the avowal: "De plus, le diable y trouvait son compte pour ce que je ne nommerai pas et que Dieu a bien voulu pardonner. Car je n'ai jamais pu distinguer la part de pureté et celle d'impureté qui se mêlaient dans mes affections." (DT, p. 164) Eventually, however, the intention of conforming his behavior to his Christian beliefs took him back to Saint-Benoît to resume the devout parish life. In 1944, at the age of sixty-eight, Jacob, wearing the yellow star of David imposed by the Nazis, was deported to the concentration camp of Drancy. He died a few weeks after his arrival. Just before internment, he wrote the following note to the priest of Saint-Benoît: "J'ai des conversions en train.... J'ai confiance en Dieu

---

[3] *Correspondance de Max Jacob,* ed. François Garnier (Paris: Editions de Paris, 1955), II, 67. Subsequent references to this edition, abbreviated *Corr.,* will be cited, hereafter, in the text.

[4] Cited by Hélène Henry, "Bio-bibliographie de Max Jacob," *Europe,* 36 (avr.-mai 1958), 117-18. André Billy, in *Max Jacob,* rev. ed., Poètes d'aujourd'hui, No. 3 (Paris: Seghers, 1945), p. 46, refers to these years as a "période de grand dandysme et de dissipation."

et dans mes amis. Je le remercie du martyre qui commence. Respectueusement et amicalement, Max Jacob. Je n'oublie personne dans mes prières quotidiennes."[5] His last written words manifest the double impulse of ironic humor and passionate faith that typifies Jacob's life and writings. This final message underscored the absurdity of obtaining Christian martyrdom through identification as a Jew ("J'ai des conversions en train") while, at the same time, it assured his Catholic confessor of the steadfastness of his orthodox practices ("mes prières quotidiennes").

With Max Jacob's death, the questions raised by his contemporaries about the authenticity of his faith recede into the domain of permanent speculation. Whether the apparition on the wall of his room was the invention of an imagination stimulated by an overdose of ether, by a crisis in a hysterical personality, by a conscious or unconscious wish for social acceptance, or whether it was indeed a mystical vision, the revelation it represented to Jacob remained fixed in the center of his consciousness.[6] Transformed into praxis through his conversion to Catholicism, the vision of a new man determined Jacob's subsequent attitude toward his existence. It also resulted in the decision to relate his writing to his spiritual evolution.

Jacob's religious beliefs were characterized by consistency amidst contradiction. While his opinions on dogma wavered, his faith had its foundation in a constant anti-rationalism. He was a mystic whose religion came to life from his visions. He believed in the invisible presence of the divine in the material world. In his Introduction to the *Défense de Tartufe*, André Blanchet compared Jacob to early Christian writers, like Saint Paul, who thought in a cosmological and spiritual framework supported by Judaïc thought. (DT, p. 21) Gabriel Bounoure, on the other hand, attached Jacob's beliefs uniquely to the doctrines of the kabbala.[7] He was refuted by Jean

---

[5] Cited by Louis Emié, *Dialogues avec Max Jacob* (Paris: Corréa, Buchet, et Chastel, 1954), p. 14.

[6] Kamber, *Max Jacob and the Poetics of Cubism*, pp. xix-xxviii, reviews several theories on the conversion.

[7] Cf. "*Les Pénitents en maillots roses; Visions infernales; Fond de l'eau; Rivages*, par Max Jacob," NRF, 43 (juill.-déc. 1934), 117: "Max Jacob est un mystique juif dont la poésie se fonde sur l'idée kabbaliste de l'emboîtement des êtres, sur la croyance qu'on s'élève au réel par franchissement de cercles concentriques."

Rousselot, who claimed that the poet's occultism was more eclectic.[8] A source neglected by these commentators, which could have provided Jacob with a model for his belief in signs, visions, and eternal archetypes, for his attempt to syncretize diverse theosophies and Christianity, as well as for his mystical dialogues, was the writing of the medieval mystic, Raymond Lull, whose *Le Livre de l'ami et de l'aimé* Jacob translated into French.[9] In view of the poet's awareness of his great-grandfather's legendary religious practices, we might even recognize an analogy between Jacob's faith and the Hasidic tradition.[10] In its rejection of logical thought, its emphasis on the penetration of the commonplace by the divine, its use of the anecdotal as a source of occult revelation, Jacob's religion embodied the characteristic traits of Hasidism.[11]

Finally, however, Jacob's mystical way was of his own invention. If his convictions exhibited an affinity with several acknowledged forms of mysticism, they were positively identified with none. There were two principal correlatives to his belief in the hidden presence of divinity in the terrestrial sphere. First of all, manifestations of the spirit belonged to one of two categories — the good or the evil. Behind the phenomena of everyday reality antagonistic moral forces perpetuated a struggle, which might be represented in Christian, kabbalistic, or astrological terms. The second corollary of Jacob's vision was the notion of communicating with invisible spiritual entities. Whether they took the form of devils, angels, genies, saints, Satan, or Christ, Jacob attempted to reach these beings through direct address.

Such was the spiritual atmosphere pervading Jacob's religious poetry. As he stated in his *Art poétique,* he sought to transform the commonplace into the miraculous: "Je rêvais de recréer la vie de la terre dans l'atmosphère du ciel." (p. 73) The following colloquy illustrates his method of poetically transposing the dominant elements of his religious spirit — the interpenetration of the divine

---

[8] *Max Jacob au sérieux* (Paris: Sûbervie, 1958), p. 164. René Plantier, *Max Jacob* (Paris: Desclée de Brouwer, 1972), pp. 22-44, has also objected to the overestimation of kabbalistic influence on Jacob's writings.

[9] Tr. A. de Barrau and Max Jacob (Paris: Editions de la Sirène, 1919).

[10] Cf. Robert Guiette, "Vie de Max Jacob," NRF, 43 (juill. 1934), 7.

[11] The affinity occurred to me, as I compared Jacob's beliefs with the tradition as depicted by Elie Wiesel, in *Célébration hassidique* (Paris: Editions du Seuil, 1972).

and the everyday, the opposition of the pure and the impure, the desire for a mystical dialogue:

> "Jésus, Notre Seigneur, est-il là?
> —N.S. n'est pas là! tous les saints sont là si vous voulez.
> —C'est au Seigneur que j'ai affaire.
> —Vous repasserez une autre fois.
> —Je n'ai pas d'autre foi.
> —Le Seigneur dit: "Frappez et on vous ouvrira!" Ça ne signifie pas qu'Il se dérange Lui-même.
> —Dites-Lui que j'attendrai patiemment.
> —Purifiez-vous! vous avez les mains et les pieds sales.
> —J'apporte la Couronne d'Epines que le Seigneur avait perdue.
> —Entrez." [12]

This text, which figures in a series of poems grouped under the title, "Actualités éternelles," presents a contradiction to which Jacob returned incessantly, in his metaphysics and his poetry: the dialectical process through which spirituality not only transfigures material objects, but is itself transfigured, or defigured, by materialization. Accordingly, the penitent "je" of the colloquy, like the convert of "Le Christ au cinématographe," has a dual nature. Although he imitates Christ by wearing the crown of thorns, he does not resist a witty *calembour* ("fois"/"foi") at the expense of his own humility. The juxtaposition of the colloquial and devotional codes, here, produces a polyvalent effect typical of Jacob's devotional poems. While elevating the familiar, it simultaneously brings the mystical down to earth.

The title of the present study, *Clown at the Altar,* comes from a list of alternative titles proposed by Max Jacob for *Les Pénitents en maillots roses.* Each of the paradigmatic substitutes suggests the antithesis of the mystical and the burlesque. (B, p. 206) At the time Jacob wrote these poems, the clown was an established archetype in literature and painting. Yet, although the theme had become a cliché, the contexts created by Jacob invested the figure with renewed poetic force. In his life and in his texts, the clown embodied the principle of contradiction. Jean Starobinski's remarks on the

---

[12] Max Jacob, "Actualités Eternelles," NRF, 43 (juill. 1934), 27.

qualities of opposition traditionally evoked by the image might be specifically applied to Jacob's concretizations of the theme: "Envol et chute, triomphe et déchéance; agilité et ataxie; gloire et immolation: le destin des figures clownesques oscille entre ces extrêmes. Parfois nous assistons à la condensation convulsive des contraires ... ailleurs prévaut l'alternance de ces états opposés; ailleurs encore il est fait appel à la ressource traditionnelle des types associés par couples dissymétriques, où chaque partenaire remplit une fonction distincte." [13] The condensation of contraries, the alternation of opposite states, the asymmetrical couple or double man, these movements of division associated with the clown motif, in Jacob's writings, reached the painful intensity of a quest for identity, as well as a salvational Passion: "Tous mes cris et tous mes écrits / au carrefour du crucifix!" (HC, p. 60)

If the clown signified antithesis, the clown at the altar was a hyperbole of contradiction, emphasizing an ironic view of the penitent as a caricature of the true convert. Just as the clown's flights of fancy are inevitably undermined by humiliating reminders of his gross physicality, Jacob's *vieux personnage* parodied the roles assumed by the new man. And in depicting the penitent as a clown, his poetry dramatized the poet's relation to the public, a society of disbelievers, to whom his mysticism appeared, at the least, anachronistic and ridiculous, or, at the worst, hypocritical and ridiculous. It is as if, through his own skeptical attitude, Jacob attempted to forestall the skepticism of others. The figure of the clown, moreover, was not the only sign of contradiction in his writing, where the interpenetrating levels of form and theme manifested a determinant pattern of antithesis. As Claude Roy remarked in his Preface to the recent edition of the *Ballades*: "La dissonance est son lieu, la rupture de ton sa constance, et son repos le mouvement perpétuel." (B, pp. 9-10) The religious poetry of Max Jacob consisted not of harmonious verses, reflecting the faith of a tranquil *dévot,* but of dynamic texts, transcribing the agitation of a Christian poet, who doubted the authenticity of his religious beliefs, his aesthetics, and his art.

---

[13] *Portrait de l'artiste en saltimbanque* (Geneva: Albert Skira, 1970), p. 101. On Jacob, Starobinski commented, p. 114: "La clownerie fut tout ensemble grimace d'humiliation et variante parodique de l'Imitation de Jésus-Christ."

Je craque de discordes militaires avec moi-même,
je me suis comme une poulie, une voiture de dilemmes.

MAX JACOB, *Sacrifice impérial*

CHAPTER I

METAPHYSICS: THEOSOPHY AND FAITH

After his conversion, Max Jacob became a devout, but not an orthodox, Catholic. Reflecting a personal vision of man and the universe, his metaphysics incorporated occult tradition as well as Christian dogma. The divergent sources of his faith produced inconsistencies resolved by Jacob in two ways — through negation and through synthesis. At times, he contradicted himself. Or else, he relied on mysticism to transcend the notion of contradiction: if all things participate in the oneness of God, then oppositions are only apparent. Mystical eclecticism sustained his attempts to synthesize beliefs drawn from the kabbala, orphism, astrology, and the Bible. Yet, in spite of the inventiveness of his religious syncretism, Jacob recognized the improbable nature of his endeavor. He admitted with regret the inadequacy of his faculties compared with his aspirations for hermeneutical knowledge.

The whole of Jacob's metaphysical system must be hypothesized from the partial views expressed in his texts on religion and in his correspondence. In June 1909, three months before his first revelation, Jacob made the earliest written allusion to his cosmology, in a letter to Guillaume Apollinaire. He presented his vision of the cosmos as a series of concentric spheres, whose microcosmic image appears in the skins of the onion:

> L'oignon, mon cher ami, sera un jour considéré comme un Dieu si l'hypothèse des cercles est acceptée. Il y a plusieurs univers, cosmiquement parlant, c'est-à-dire des ensembles inimaginables de forces interchangeables minutieusement et intérieurement. Malgré tout ce que nous

> inventons, comme disent ces Messieurs, pour éviter notre misérable relativité... hum!... nous ne pouvons donc qu'ignorer les influences que nous subissons.
>
> ... ...
>
> En conclusion, mon cher ami, quand l'oignon sera l'objet d'un culte, quand l'oignon sera le raccourci de l'univers, quand on considérera comme il faudrait, le ciel aussi bien comme temps et comme espace, dans toutes dimensions possibles...[1]

His hyperbolic conclusion, however, suggesting the divine cult of the onion, gave the exposition an ironic overtone.

Throughout Jacob's writings, the figure of concentric circles recurs as a symbol of the cosmos. In a proselytizing letter of 1941, sent to Louis Emié, a young poet disciple, Jacob still employed the onion as a cosmological image. But this time the context was serious. The letter reveals the moral implications of Jacob's vision, for it associated the spheres of the universe with heaven and hell and situated the soul in one or another of these zones:

> Où est situé l'enfer? Connais-tu ces jouets chinois où une petite boîte est dans une boîte plus grande, et celle-ci dans une autre à l'infini? c'est l'image des mondes. Ils s'emboîtent les uns dans les autres sans que nos sens à l'ordinaire aient la capacité de les apercevoir.... L'enfer coexiste avec des apparences différentes, nous sommes enveloppés dans ces pelures d'oignons et notre âme qui n'est pas terrestre appartient déjà à l'une de ces pelures et *l'habite déjà* alors qu'elle paraît être avec notre corps. Nous sommes déjà à l'enfer ou au Paradis.[2]

From the center of Jacob's concentric worlds radiated divinity; towards the periphery the zones became increasingly material and morally inferior: "Tout se répète et les catégories s'étendent à l'infini du meilleur au pire dans le cosmos."[3]

One of the firmest tenets of Jacob's metaphysics was the belief in the presence of the divine in the everyday. For Jacob, no object

---

[1] *Correspondance de Max Jacob,* ed. François Garnier (Paris: Editions de Paris, 1953), I, 34-35. Subsequent references to this edition, abbreviated *Corr.,* will be cited, hereafter, in the text.

[2] Emié, p. 201.

[3] Cited by Pierre Lagarde, *Max Jacob, mystique et martyr* (Paris: Editions Baudinière, 1944), p. 68.

or event was neutral. Commonplace phenomena, like the onion and the Chinese toy boxes, were charged with hidden meaning. Thus, he insisted that his terrestrial surroundings embodied the moral spheres of Paradise, Hell, and Purgatory: "Ces mondes coexistent en un même point sans s'apercevoir. Ainsi peuvent coexister la Terre, les Paradis, les Enfers, le Purgatoire, invisibles et présents. Je crois que sur la terre nous pouvons déjà appartenir à l'un de ces mondes et même au monde de la terre. Le monde de l'enfer, j'y crois, j'en ai vu des échantillons sur la terre, dans les villes, parmi les brutes des faubourgs et des banlieues, les femmes ivrognesses, les enfants martyrs."[4] Identification of these signs, nevertheless, often became problematic: "Or ce n'est qu'aujourd'hui que je me souviens de ce prêtre qui n'était point un prêtre mais un artifice de Satan." (B, p. 52) For the symbols of the heavenly and infernal zones were not always obvious and not always constant.

Jacob derived his cosmology chiefly from the kabbala, which he claimed to have studied "énormément," in the translation of Jean de Pauly.[5] In the *Zohar*, or *Book of Splendor*, Jacob found the figure of concentric circles (in the variants of an onion, a fruit, a nut, a brain) representing the form of the cosmos. His metaphor of the soul enveloped in the peels of an onion corresponded to the kabbalistic image of man's spirit surrounded by inferior material coverings, in a structure analogous to the universal order:

> A partir du mystérieux Point suprême jusqu'au plus infime degré de la création, tout sert de vêtement à quelque autre chose, et cette autre chose sert de vêtement à une chose supérieure, et ainsi de suite. *De sorte que* le cerveau entouré d'une pelure sert, lui-même de pelure à un cerveau supérieur; tout est donc cerveau à ce qui lui est inférieur et pelure à ce qui lui est supérieur. Le Point suprême projetait une lumière immense d'une telle limpidité, d'une telle transparence et d'une telle subtilité qu'elle pénétra partout. De cette façon se forma autour de ce Point un palais lui servant de vêtement. La lumière du Point suprême étant

---

[4] Cited by Lagarde, p. 68.
[5] See, Yvon Belaval, *La Rencontre avec Max Jacob* (Paris: Charlot, 1946), p. 47; and Max Jacob, *Lettres à Marcel Béalu*, preceded by *Dernier visage de Max Jacob*, by Marcel Béalu (Lyon: Emmanuel Vitte, 1959), p. 122. Subsequent references to the latter edition, abbreviated *Lettres*, will be cited, hereafter, in the text.

> d'une subtilité inconcevable, celle du palais qui lui est inférieure forme ainsi un cercle foncé autour de lui. Mais la lumière du premier palais, bien qu'inférieure à celle du Point suprême, étant cependant d'une splendeur immense, a fini par former autour de ce palais un autre qui lui sert *en quelque sorte* de vêtement, et ainsi de suite; *ainsi*, à partir du Point suprême, toutes les échelles de la création ne sont que des pelures les unes aux autres; la pelure de l'échelle supérieure forme le cerveau de l'échelle inférieure. Cet ordre d'en haut a été également constitué ici-bas, *ainsi* qu'il est écrit: "Et Elohim créa l'homme à son image"; car l'homme est composé de cerveau et de méninges, d'esprit et de corps; tout cela est nécessaire à l'ordre du monde." [6]

According to the kabbalistic cosmogony, God first manifested himself in the form of a luminous point, from which emanated an Archetypal, Heavenly Man, referred to as the World of Emanation and composed of ten immaterial entities called the ten *Sephira*. [7] From the Archetypal Man, also known as the kabbalistic tree, emanated the worlds of the universe: the World of Creation inhabited by the king of the angels, the World of Formation, inhabited by angels and heavenly bodies, and the World of Matter, inhabited by the grosser elements, the abode of inferior angels in which darkness and impurity increase with the descent of each degree. Jacob, like the kabbalists, conceived of man as the microcosm of the Archetypal Man, as literally containing cosmic worlds within his body.

In spite of correspondences between his vision and kabbalistic cosmology, Jacob exercised imaginative freedom in elaborating his metaphysics. His idea of the "Ciel des Images," syncretizing elements drawn from Greek orphism, the Bible, and the kabbala, constituted a personal explanation of dreams and prophecies. This theory was essential to his poetics, for it supported his conception of inspiration. In an article entitled "La Clef des songes" (1925), Jacob connected the Christian belief in the immanence and tran-

---

[6] *Sepher Ha-Zohar (Le Livre de la Splendeur)*, tr. Jean de Pauly (Paris: Ernest Leroux, 1906), I, 122. Italics indicate phrases added by the translator.

[7] For a concise summary of the kabbalistic cosmogony, see Christian D. Ginsburg, *The Kabbalah, Its Doctrines, Development, and Literature* (London: George Routledge & Sons Limited, 1920).

scendance of God to both the kabbalistic belief in spiritual spheres and the ancient occult notion of eternal forms. By ingeniously modifying the standard interpretation of a line from Psalm 142 (143), he pretended to derive his visionary hypothesis directly from Biblical exegesis:

> *Anxiatus est SUPER ME spiritus meus.* Si l'on admet que l'esprit est hors de l'homme (ce qui n'empêche pas l'âme d'être en lui *in me conturbatum est cor meum*) si l'on admet l'existence des ciels on a l'explication des rêves et des visions prophétiques. D'après la Tradition occultiste dont Platon a, paraît-il, fait souvent profiter ses théories, le ciel le plus proche de nous, le neuvième ciel, le ciel de la Lune est aussi le Ciel des Images: là nous nous trouvons figurés avec nos actes, avant pendant et après eux. Le ciel de la Lune est un ciel de clichés. [8]

Having assumed the interpenetration of the human and divine spirit, Jacob went on to explain the nature of the prophet's (or poet's) communication with the world of eternal images or *clichés*. [9] Ordinarily the spiritual zones of the cosmos remained imperceptible: "Les mondes sont separés non par des abîmes matériels, mais par des impossibilités matérielles de se connaître par les sens humains." [10] Yet, under exceptional circumstances, the mind could visualize the cosmic order. Fever, dreams, drugs, the traditional visionary methods, were those prescribed by Jacob: "Nos sens peuvent être augmentés (ou diminués) de telle sorte que nous parvenons à sortir de notre monde (la fièvre, le sommeil, les poisons peuvent nous sortir de notre monde). Cette sortie s'opère par osmose." [11] About the

---

[8] *Philosophies*, 1ʳᵉ ann. (janv.-mars 1924-25), 577. Subsequent references to this article, abbreviated "*Cds,*" will be cited, hereafter, in the text. Although Jacob's citation of Ps. 142(143) 1.4 was exact, his personal interpretation of "SUPER ME," as signifying the situation of the spirit outside of man, did not correspond with standard French versions of the line. Cf. *La Sainte Bible*, tr. Osterwald (Paris: Comité de la Société biblique de France, 1904): "Et mon esprit est abbatu en moi; mon cœur est troublé au dedans de moi."

[9] Jacob, famous for his *jeux de mots*, undoubtedly, chose the term "cliché" for its polysemic value, since both its literal meanings signifying plastic form (a plate of type; an illustration block; a photographic negative) and its figurative sense connoting intellectual form (a stereotyped phrase) apply in the context of images supposed to inspire prophets and poets.

[10] Cited by Lagarde, p. 68.

[11] Cited by Emié, p. 201. "Poisons" probably signified "drugs" to Jacob,

obstacles encountered by the mystic, however, Jacob was emphatic. The state of contemplation, first of all, required a paradoxical attitude of passive attentiveness: "Evidemment les mots 'état d'attente' ne signifient pas du tout que le sujet attend des visions. Même! l'inattendu est une condition de la valeur de la vision." ("*Cds,*" pp. 580-81) Even after achieving contact with the "Ciel des Images," the visionary did not necessarily decipher the significance of the prophetic images: "Des gens soumis aux mêmes circonstances, aux mêmes influences voient sans s'être convertés les mêmes formes prophétiques. Il est difficile de tirer des prédictions de ces formes parce que dans le ciel des Images les événements les plus minces figurent à côté des plus graves et que rien ne souligne ceux-ci." ("*Cds,*" p. 578) Rational interpretation faltered, because human categories of value, such as the constructs of time and space, did not exist in the eternal sphere of spiritual unity.

Through dreams and visions, Jacob believed, man might communicate with spirits. Although he followed kabbalistic theosophy in literally identifying these beings as inhabitants of the cosmic circles, Jacob referred to them in the Christian terminology of devils and angels and, correspondingly, defined their moral qualities. In "La Clef des songes," the description of his visionary experience employed traditional Christian demonic imagery: "Les visions d'origine démoniaque sont aisément reconnaissables: dans les personnages figurés se mêlent des parties animales. Parfois ils sont infirmes, servent de béquilles, ils ont de longues queues. Ils ont le plus souvent de très petites mains, de très petits pieds et souvent la figure voilée. Parfois de très petites têtes dont l'expression est froide et féroce." (p. 581)[12] But these entities possessed the power of metamorphosis, so that recognizing their nature could be difficult:

---

who admitted having taken ether in attempts to recreate his first vision, but denied having taken it previous to his revelation. (DT, p. 109, p. 157) Jacob's biographical commentators, however, generally agree that he used drugs prior to September 1909.

[12] The Christian mystic's revulsion for temptations of the flesh is commonly projected as the physical deformity of the devil, as in Sainte Thérèse de Jésus, *Œuvres complètes,* tr. Les Carmélites du premier monastère de Paris (Paris: Beauchesne & Cie., 1907), p. 399: "Un jour que je me trouvais dans un oratoire, il m'apparut à mon côté gauche, sous une forme hideuse. Tandis qu'il me parlait, je remarquai sa bouche: elle était épouvantable." And, p. 400: "Je vis près de moi un affreux petit nègre, qui grinçait des dents."

"Les anges sont des émanations planétaires pas plus malins que des hommes; il faut donc discuter, en s'appuyant sur Dieu, leurs pauvres inspirations. Il y a des anges remarquables aussi; il faut les mériter, ou bien les recevoir de la bonté de Dieu. Il y a des démons inspirateurs de vols, de crimes, d'entêtement. Il faut prier Dieu de vous en débarrasser." (CJP, p. 27) As a Christian mystic, then, Jacob was under injunction to repudiate infernal visions.

With the practice of astrology, Jacob reinforced his belief in the duality of visible and invisible worlds, in the presence of the divine in the everyday. Identifying the kabbalistic spheres with the material bodies of the solar system, he inferred the direct influence of occult forces upon his daily existence: "Les ciels ont leurs correspondances sur la terre; ils ont reçu des noms de planètes depuis l'antiquité; on attribue à ce que représentent ces noms de planètes des affinités avec certains jours, certaines couleurs, certaines heures, certains pays, certains temps, certains objets." ("*Cds*," p. 582) His preface to a work by Conrad Moricand, with whom he later collaborated in writing *Le Miroir de l'astrologie,* praised the author for having reversed the usual astrological approach — "avec la force et la couleur d'un vrai créateur" — by basing his characterology upon actual psychological observation.[13] Jacob encouraged creativity, even in the preparation of horoscopes. Thus, in a letter to a young poet, verbal play and ironic allusions to "café astrologists" deliberately exposed his preference for invention: "Je préparais ton horoscope pour ton anniversaire.... Il est troublant, comme toi-même et je serai bien tenté — est-ce le démon — d'y mettre du mien.... Ton Bélier n'est pas bêlant ni belliqueux: Mars n'a rien à y voir. Je ne parle pas, ce serait moins orthodoxe, de l'influence des Poissons d'Avril sensible pour les astrologues de café. Mais je n'en suis pas, Monsieur!" (*Corr.,* I, 187) Because of his unorthodoxy, he could reconcile astrology with the Catholic doctrine of free will: "A quelque tentation qu'un astre nous expose, l'âme a les mêmes droits et les mêmes devoirs. L'astrologie ne supprime pas les tribunaux, elle pourrait les éclairer."[14] In effect, this dubious compromise parodied theological arguments accommodating Christian free will and predetermination.

---

[13] *Les Interprètes* (Paris: Editions de la Sirène, 1919), p. ii.
[14] *Ibid.,* p. iii.

To synthesize his divergent religious beliefs, Jacob habitually relied upon the medieval science of symbolism, practiced extensively by the kabbalists. In the period immediately following his revelation, he sought the esoteric meaning of his apparition through analyses that employed a method of theosophic syncretism. Interpreting the significance of the red-colored tapestry upon which the "Corps Céleste" had appeared, Jacob referred to planetary intervention: "Le rouge est une couleur du ciel de Mars.... Cette couleur avait son expression dans l'ensemble significatif: elle convenait au temps dans lequel l'apparition avait lieu: elle voulait exprimer que la révolution qu'elle apportait était due à l'epoque naissante alors du règne du ciel de Mars." ("*Cds*," p. 582) Another interpretation of the vision combined Christian mysticism (the figurative reading of the Bible) with a traditional esoteric view of phenomena (the symbolism of colors and parts of the body): "Je n'entendis point la voix du Seigneur mais, plus tard, je compris Ses Signes. Ce que j'appris de la Sainte Face, des Saintes Epaules, et aussi, du jaune et du bleu m'instruisit des rapports entre la Robe Divine ce jour-là, Son Très Sacré Corps adorable et ma carrière d'artiste." [15]

In the unpublished manuscript entitled "L'Anatomie religieuse" or "La Symbolique des Evangiles," Jacob pursued this attempt to fuse occult Tradition and the Bible. Along with scriptural exegesis, he adopted the kabbalistic technique of deciphering numbers: "Quand il s'agit de la colombe, c'est-à-dire, de la réconciliation, Noë l'attend 7 jours. 7 étant un nombre de paix et amour. Tel est l'esprit sous lequel il faudrait comprendre l'ancien testament." [16] In the spirit of the kabbala, Jacob also assumed the phonetic similarity of signifiers implied an analogy between the objects signified. [17] Accordingly, he discerned Noah's prefiguration of Moses through the linguistic equivalence of two signs: "Le même mot 'Jebah' signifie l'arche de Noë et la petite nacelle de papyrus où fut placé Moïse enfant sur le Nil." ("*Anat.*," MS. 8140-233) Like the kabbalistic

---

[15] MS. 7198-4, p. 7. This manuscript entitled "Différents états d'esprit, ou portrait de l'auteur... au travail" is dated "juin 1917-mai 1918" and located in the Jacques Doucet Collection, Paris.

[16] "L'Anatomie religieuse," MS. 8140-405. This manuscript is located in the Jacques Doucet Collection, at the Bibliothèque Sainte-Geneviève, Paris. Subsequent references, abbreviated "*Anat.*," will be cited, hereafter, in the text.

[17] Cf. Jacob's view of the nature of language, below, p. 47.

works, the "Anatomie religieuse" emphasized mystical correspondences linking the Old and New Testaments, Christianity and Antiquity. For example, while extolling the inspirational powers of wine, Jacob adapted current anthropological theories to focus on the prophetic relation of Egyptian and Greek mysteries to Christian revelation:

> A la vérité l'abus du vin n'a la plupart du temps pas d'autre cause que le désir de jouir de tous ses esprits, chez un être trop faible pour les tenir autrement. Quoiqu'il en soit le vin et l'esprit sont associés et depuis toujours. Osiris est en Egypte un Dieu civilisateur et aussi le planteur de la vigne, je crois bien. Si j'étais savant je trouverais certes dans l'Inde et en Chine quelque autre dieu qui corroberait mon dire. Je m'en tiens à ce que tout le monde sait sur Dyonisios ou Bacchus qui fut pour les grecs à la fois l'inventeur de la vigne, et aussi l'inventeur du dithyrambe du théâtre. Bacchus présidait à des "mystères"; je pense que ces "mystères" devaient être quelque chose comme les "Initiations" à des sciences qui furent jadis des pressentiments de la vérité christique. Dans leurs actuelles subsistances aujourd'hui ils sont les marques d'un orgueil qui, sans pouvoir oublier les Evangiles, prétendent pourtant se passer de leurs enseignments. ("*Anat.*," MS. 8140-178)

Of course, the "sciences," equated in an afterthought with the sin of pride, were the occult practices in which, at the very moment, Jacob was engaged!

The suggestive title of the "Anatomie religieuse" points to a dominant concern in Jacob's metaphysics. A number of his mystical beliefs attempted to eliminate the antithesis of anatomy and religion, that is, of matter and spirit. Ultimately, Jacob accomplished the reconciliation through Christian faith in the sacrament of communion: "Ma chair est esprit et vie dit le Seigneur. Toute sa chair est esprit et vie de l'esprit. Et Dieu est homme.... Il est donc un résumé de tout l'Esprit de l'Humanité par ses membres de chair divine. En se sacrifiant, c'est donc chacun de nous qui s'est sacrifié en sa Personne. Participer à la messe, c'est donc participer au Sacrifice de toute Intelligence Humaine et Divine possible et profiter de ce Sacrifice." ("*Anat.*," MS. 8140-78) But his insistence on uncovering the precise spiritual sense of all parts of the anatomy — "Tous les membres sont donc esprit" (*idem*) — reflected the kabbalistic view of man, the microcosm of the Archetypal Man, whose members encompassed cosmic worlds. In his analyses of man's physical nature, moreover, Jacob's personal motivations were often apparent, notably the guilt occasioned by his homosexuality. Considering that Jacob was bald at an early age, his interpretation of long hair implied his own moral degeneration: "Longs cheveux, innocence. Les cheveux sont le siège des affûts inspirateurs. Avoir gardé la chevelure, c'est avoir gardé le caractère de l'enfance." ("*Anat.*," MS. 8140-74) And the connotation of sexual prohibition was implicit in the following anatomical interpretation embellished with astrological allusions: "La chair devait être lacérée parce que la chair c'est la vie, c'est Vénus (augmentation nature) mais les os ne devaient pas être rompus car l'os est Saturne, esprit, continuation, durée." ("*Anat.*," MS. 8214-15) One of his analyses accords strikingly with a classical Freudian archetype. This is the explanation of Judith cutting off the head of Holofernes as the prefiguration of the Virgin "detruisant la puissance du démon." ("*Anat.*," MS. 8140-98) If decapitation symbolizes castration, then Jacob was equating the male sexual organ with the principle of evil.[18]

Symbolism, the synthesis of mystical beliefs, prophetic visions, these orphic endeavors manifested Jacob's passionate attachment to theosophy. And yet, he considered them heretical. In an unpublished manuscript entitled "Différents états d'esprit," he explicitly set forth his reservations: "Mon habilité dans l'interprétation des symboles me donnait le goût de m'y exercer. Ce goût porté sur les Ecritures Saintes puis par l'habitude sur les moindres circonstances devint de suite une superstition tragique. On trouverait par la crise morale de *Victor Matorel* celle qui fut la mienne mais plus particulièrement par l'"Anatomie Religieuse" livre hérétique qu'un chrétien ne peut publier l'attachement à moi de la Symbolique dont je ne suis pas encore délivré."[19] Within the "Anatomie" itself, as indicated by his condemnatory remark concluding the passage on the spiritual meaning of wine, appeared signs of self-repudiation. A dialogue between "l'auteur" and "le démon des bibliothèques (il

---

[18] For Sigmund Freud's analysis of decapitation as a castration symbol, see, *The Interpretation of Dreams*, tr. A. A. Brill (New York: Macmillan, 1933), p. 346.

[19] MS. 7198-4, p. 6.

est femme)" parodied the practice of symbolism. Its grotesque depiction of Buddhist statues, its humorous equation of Descartes with Mohammed, and the absurdity of its symbolic explication, presented by the devil, convey the writer's ironic attitude toward occultism:

Le démon

Je vais te donner une première idée de la méthode bouddhique. Les statuaires orientaux figurent le sage avec des oreilles longues.

L'auteur

J'ai vu cela... au... le lobe arrive à la hauteur de la bouche sans doute pour définir que l'on doit écouter avant de parler.

Le démon

Pas si innocents les bouddhistes, mon jeune ami! laisse donc ses sottises à Mahomet, le Descartes de l'Est! ce n'est pas cela!... Le bas de la figure est réservé à la volonté; or la Volonté ne compte pas dans la Religion de la Lune. Le Haut de la Figure avec la bosse qui remplace notre Golgotha forme vis à vis de la bouche un triangle dont les oreilles sont les pointes. ("*Anat.*," MS. 8214-115)

Lending further credence to his statement that a Christian could not publish the "Anatomie religieuse," Jacob, in fact, did not seek publication of the manuscript.

His disavowal of orphic "superstition" suggests possibly a spiritual evolution. Both André Blanchet and René Plantier have presented evidence of the increasing orthodoxy of Jacob's faith. According to Blanchet's Introduction to the *Défense de Tartufe*, the poet rejected the search for occult knowledge after his baptism; he systematically reduced allusions to the kabbala in narrations of his revelation. (DT, p. 60) It is indeed a fact that the *Défense*'s dedication identified mysticism with a phase of the author's metaphysical life transcended by Catholic piety. Surveying the themes of Jacob's writings, Plantier found the quest for the absolute gradually dominated by the acceptance of human limits and the belief in redemption through Christ.[20] Perhaps the most convincing testament of the poet's movement in that direction was his daily religious meditation. While reflecting on the themes prescribed by Saint François in the *Introduction à la vie dévote* — the Creation, the End for which we are created, the Blessings of God, Sin, Death, Judgment, Hell, Paradise, the election of Paradise, the election of the devout life — Jacob expressed sentiments of humility and repentance, fear of death, and hope for salvation:

> J'ai confiance que le soleil se lèvera demain et aussi confiance que vous me permettrez de vous avoir tout à l'heure dans la Sainte Hostie. Quelle bénédiction que cette Sainte et Divine Hostie qui raffermit ma foi, me délivre de l'enfer. Combien je me sens pécheur abominable en m'approchant de ce Sacrement si sacré, et en constatant mon peu de progrès vers Vous.[21]

In such meditations, the conflict of opposing desires ("prier" versus "comprendre") uncovered in the *Défense* by Blanchet, was repeatedly decided in favor of prayer.

As Jacob fortified his adherence to Catholic dogma, the occult tradition continued, nonetheless, to attract him. The spiritual evolution announced in the *Défense*'s dedicatory remarks, after all, figured in a fictional confession.[22] Even Blanchet affirmed that Jacob, in spite of his official orthodox commitment, "ne renoncera jamais à une forme de pensée qui nous est devenu étrangère et qui nous déconcerte." (DT, p. 22) Indeed, it was after his baptism and retreat to Saint Benoît that he elaborated the visionary theory of the "Ciel des Images," as well as new representations of his cosmology. As late as 1937, he declared of the kabbala: "C'est une métaphysique,

---

[20] *Max Jacob*, p. 48. A similar hypothesis regarding the poet's spiritual evolution was set forth by Pierre Andreu, *Max Jacob* (Paris: Wesmael-Charlier, 1962), p. 121: "Max, qui l'avait tenté avant son baptême — c'est la periode "mystique" de la *Défense de Tartuffe* [sic] — savait qu'il est vain d'espérer atteindre la vie surnaturelle, la pleine vie chrétienne, sans l'aide des sacrements, c'est-à-dire sans les prêtres qui les dispensent et sans l'Eglise."

[21] Max Jacob, *Méditations,* ed. René Plantier (Paris: Gallimard, 1972), p. 80. Jacob's meditations have been published in the works of his commentators (see, Andreu, Belaval, Emié, Lagarde), in *La Défense de Tartufe,* and in Max Jacob, *Méditations religieuses* (Paris: Gallimard, 1947).

[22] Cf. My discussion of the autobiographical authenticity of the *Défense,* below, pp. 72-73.

la seule métaphysique et, je crois, la base de toutes les religions."
(*Lettres*, p. 122) And in 1939, dictating the final account of his conversion to the Abbé Foucher, an official of the Church, Jacob not only mentioned his early occult practices without disparagement — "Je me résignais à n'être pas baptisé, je m'en consolais en lisant l'Ancien et le Nouveau Testament. Les lumières que j'avais acquises en symbolique, alors que j'étudiais cette science pour essayer de comprendre le sens de ma vision, donnaient à cette étude un remarquable interêt." (DT, p. 293) — but also boasted of the visions he still occasionally received: "Mais à quoi bon parler de ces images? Ne faudrait-il pas mentionner celles que j'accueille encore parfois en ces soixante années de mon âge?" (DT, p. 291) Finally, in a letter of 1941 to Yvon Belaval, he called the teachings of the kabbala "la seule philosophie *vraie*." [23]

After his conversion, Jacob's first enterprise was to synthesize theosophy and Catholic faith. But when he realized that mystical syntheses, such as those of the "Anatomie religieuse," were incompatible with strict orthodoxy, he denounced the practice and repented his heresy. Still, he invented new symbolical exegeses of the Bible, continued to interpret everyday events symbolically, and extolled the kabbala and the wisdom of mystics. So that, eventually, he again confronted contradictions. But the antithesis of occult and orthodox beliefs in Jacob's metaphysics was only one manifestation of a significant pattern informing his life and his writings: the consciousness of division, the attempt to eradicate it, the renewed sense of opposition.

---

[23] Belaval, p. 45.

La poésie n'a rien à voir avec les définitions, même de l'esthétique.

Max Jacob, *Lettres*

Je ne cesse de répéter à tous mes frères cadets: Méditez sur l'esthétique. Réfléchissez aux conditions du beau."

Max Jacob, *Esthétique*

CHAPTER II

POETIC THEORIES AND MYSTICISM

Max Jacob's reputation as an aesthetician ensued primarily from his contributions to the aesthetics of cubism. The most frequently cited of his theoretical texts, the 1916 Preface to his *Cornet à dés*, applied the cubist conception of painting to poetics, by defining the prose poem as "un objet construit." (p. 17) An object isolated from everyday reality: "Une œuvre d'art vaut par elle-même et non par les confrontations qu'on en peut faire avec la réalité." (CD, p. 17) In their emphasis on the autonomy of the work of art, Jacob and the other theoreticians of cubism followed the symbolist movement of the late nineteenth century. Collectively elaborating their aesthetics between about 1905 and 1920, the cubist painters and poets assumed the symbolists' antipathy to an imitative theory of art, similarly asserted the freedom of the artist to invent individualistic rules of beauty, and equally disdained intellectualism in poetry.[1] At the same time, they repudiated a dominant trait of symbolist poetics, namely, the use of a rarefied vocabulary and abstruse syntax. The evocation of commonplace objects was a first principle of

---

[1] For statements by other cubists, see Guillaume Apollinaire, "L'Esprit nouveau et les poètes," *Mercure de France*, 130 (déc. 1918), 385-96, and *Méditations esthétiques, Les Peintres cubistes* (Paris: Figuière, 1913); Georges Braque, "Thoughts and Reflections on Art," *Artists on Art*, ed. Robert Goldwater and Marco Trèves (New York, 1945), rpt. in *Theories of Modern Art: A Source Book by Artists and Critics*, ed. Herschel Chipp (Berkeley, Calif., 1968); Albert Gleizes and Jean Metzinger, *Cubism* (London, 1913), rpt. in Chipp; Daniel-Henry Kahnweiler, *Juan Gris, sa vie, son œuvre, ses écrits* (Paris: Gallimard, 1946). My general remarks on symbolism in this chapter are supported by A. G. Lehmann's thorough study, *The Symbolist Aesthetic in France (1885-1895)*, 2nd ed. (Oxford: Basil Blackwell, 1968).

cubism, and Jacob, like Apollinaire, urged poets to use ordinary language, to open themselves to the phenomena of modern life: "Enrichis-toi d'impressions de la vie... Enrichis ton vocabulaire; un poète doit *se servir de tous les mots usuels.*" [2] Nevertheless, these concrete impressions were to be detached from their naturalistic sources and transposed imaginatively in the poem. [3]

While commentators have studied in detail Jacob's cubist formulations, his ideas on the mystical nature, function, and method of poetic creation are generally ignored. [4] The Preface to the *Cornet* posited art as a synonym of style, defining both as self-projection through chosen techniques: "La volonté de s'extérioriser par des moyens choisis." (p. 15) Yet this definition did not entirely satisfy Jacob. In opposition to his cubist insistence upon fabrication and pure aesthetic enjoyment, many of his statements attributed to poetry a spiritual value deriving from its capacity to transmit intuitive knowledge of divinity. Thus, the following one-line poem from the *Cornet* evokes the second level of reality revealed by the poet: "Le mystère est dans cette vie, la réalité dans l'autre; si vous m'aimez, si vous m'aimez, je vous ferai voir la réalité." (p. 65) The underlying assumptions of Jacob's poetic mysticism corresponded to the romantic and symbolist view of the poet as pariah, prophet, and seer, hypostatized in Verlaine's well known epithet *poètes maudits.* Jacob gave these ideas an original embodiment by synthesizing them with his metaphysical notions. As a result of this integration, however, the contradictions disseminated among his religious beliefs infiltrated his poetics.

Besides collecting statements on poetry in an *Art poétique* (1922) and in the *Conseils à un jeune poète* (1945), Jacob dispersed his poetic theories in prefaces, articles for small reviews, and letters

---

[2] *Esthétique de Max Jacob,* ed. René-Guy Cadou (Paris: P. Seghers, 1956), p. 29. This collection contains comments on poetry selected from Jacob's letters to Cadou; future references to this edition, abbreviated *Esth.,* will be cited in the text.

[3] Thus, Jacob wrote to Jacques Doucet: "Vous avez déjà compris, cher Monsieur, que j'ai horreur du naturalisme, du réalisme et de toute œuvre qui ne vaut que par la comparaison qu'on peut faire avec le réel." (*Corr.,* I, 133)

[4] Cf. G. T. Harris, "André Malraux et l'Esthétique de Max Jacob," MLR, 66 (1971), 565-67; and Annette Thau, "The Esthetic Reflections of Max Jacob," FR, 45 (1972), 800-12.

to friends.[5] These writings, frequently aphoristic in form and circumstantial in motivation, exhibited both inconsistency and continuity. Instead of evolving from one aesthetic system to another, Jacob's poetics maintained consistent oppositions. For the antithetical tendencies (mystical and cubist, occult and Catholic orthodox) that marked his early thoughts on poetry recurred at each stage of his career and in his final *Conseils*.

Jacob's mystical conception of poetic revelation correlated with his kabbalistic view of language. The kabbalists, like modern linguists, distinguished in the word a triple reality: the *signe*, the *signifié*, the *signifiant*. But for mystics, the relationship of these elements remains ambivalent. While Jacob promulgated a necessary connection between the sign and the object signified (in contradiction to accepted linguistic theory of their arbitrary relation), he also perceived the ability of the sign to produce meanings independent of its referent. The basis of his intimate (non-arbitrary) association of the *signe* and the *signifié* was the kabbalistic explanation of the creation in Genesis, which assumed that the Word literally generated the cosmos. In the cosmogony of the kabbala, the original transformation of light or spirit into matter occurred precisely at the moment when the name of the Lord resounded for the first time.[6] After the Word (name of God) came into existence, its letters recombined to engender new phenomena. As a consequence of his belief in these primordial bonds, Jacob assumed verbal analogies to entail hidden relations between objects. His "Anatomie religieuse" illustrated this attitude, for example, in the assertion that Noah's arc and Moses's raft were notionally related because of the equivalence of their signs. (See above, p. 36)

In Jacob's mind, the metaphor of the world and the book was a literal fact. He could fathom the meaning of signs by contemplating the objects they signified, or divine the secrets of the universe through verbal operations. This kabbalistic power of words was formulated in a letter to Marcel Béalu:

---

[5] In letters of 1941, Jacob mentioned to Béalu the "conseils" he had written for the aspiring young poet, Jacques Evrard, and of Manoll's interest in publishing them. (*Lettres*, p. 231) However, they were eventually published posthumously by Gallimard, in 1945.

[6] *Zohar*, I, 92.

> —Aime le mot. Il faut aimer le mot. La Kabbale enseigne que la couronne de Dieu, ce sont les vingt-deux lettres de l'Alphabet sacré et que l'univers produit par le verbe n'est qu'un livre (ceci non poétiquement) car tout est nombre et le nombre est la lettre. Tout se réduit donc à la lettre, et quelques lettres sont la synthèse du monde. Vois donc l'importance des mots. (*Lettres*, p. 121)

Objects had numerical equivalents corresponding to letters, which combined to form the book embodying, for Jacob, the knowledge Mallarmé called the "explication orphique de la Terre." [7] For Mallarmé's *Divagations* had intimated the hermetical value of words, "Le Mystère dans les lettres":

> Il doit y avoir quelque chose d'occulte au fond de tous, je crois décidément à quelque chose d'abscons, signifiant fermé et caché, qui habite le commun: car, sitôt cette masse jetée vers quelque trace que c'est une réalité, existant, par exemple, sur une feuille de papier, dans tel écrit — pas en soi — cela qui est obscure: elle s'agite, ouragan jaloux d'attribuer les ténèbres à quoi que ce soit, profusément, flagramment. [8]

The ambivalence of this theory in respect to language derives from its uncertainty in defining the relation of the sign to the object signified. On the one hand, the connotations attributed by Jacob to arrangements of words (*signifiants*) were independent of the referential sense of the component signs. And yet, Jacob, like the kabbalists, insisted on inferring from these connotive meanings the actual correspondence of the referents denoted (*signifiés*).

What were the poetic implications of the mystical potential assigned to language? According to Jacob's cosmology, objects concealed spiritual significations. If the sign were equated with its referent, then the poem took on the dimension of an occult object, whose contemplation afforded divine knowledge. From this viewpoint, the images of a poem could be interpreted in the manner of verbal emblems. Illustrative of that approach were Jacob's interpretations, in the *Miroir d'astrologie,* of the verbal symbols representing each zodiacal period. For Gemini, he depicted "*une femme*

---

[7] Stéphane Mallarmé, *Propos sur la poésie*, rev. ed. (Monaco: Editions du Rocher, 1953), p. 143.

[8] (Genève: Les Editions du Mont-Blanc, 1943), p. 286.

nouant des fleurs et des rubans" and deciphered the image as "(spiritualité et savoir-faire)"; for Pisces, "*un ange entouré de flammes* (ce qui traduit l'amour de la spiritualité au milieu des déboires, des embûches, quelquefois des malheurs)"; for Cancer, "un enfant qui s'enfuit en lançant des flèches (toute puissance des sentiments favorisant le bien comme le mal)." [9] Analogous symbolical decoding occurred in the *Défense de Tartufe* and the *Visions infernales,* where titles, such as "Démons dans les formes naturelles," indicated the latent meaning of tableaux evoked in prose poems. (B, p. 65) With his *calembours,* too, Jacob sometimes suggested kabbalistic theory. For instance, the spiritual significance of "mes grelots" became manifest only through an analysis and recombination of phonetic elements: "Mes grelots! maigre lot! ce sont ceux du péché." (B, p. 56) [10] This symbolical view of language, moreover, provided quasi-scientific support for Jacob's intuitive belief that poetry united matter and spirit.

As an occult object, the poem's function was to reveal the supernatural, and Jacob signified that poetic capacity by the terms "situation" and "transplantation." [11] In respect to its mystical affect, he considered Mallarmé's poetry exemplary: "J'admire profondément Mallarmé, non par son lyrisme, mais pour la 'situation divinement géographique' de son œuvre. J'entends par situation de l'œuvre cette

---

[9] Max Jacob and Claude Valence [Conrad Moricand], 5th ed. (Paris: Gallimard, 1949), p. 56. These examples expose Jacob's double view of language, for his "symbolical" exegeses seem to equally explicate the meanings of the signs emanating from their syntagmatic arrangement. His poetry, in fact, relied more often on the extension of significance through verbal associations than through reference to fixed symbols. For example, similar expressive techniques structure the gratuitous images of the *Cornet à dés* and the personally symbolic images of the *Visions infernales.*

[10] In this context, two meanings of "grelots" apply: the literal allusion to 'carnival bells' and the popular, figurative sense of 'testicles.'

[11] Because Jacob employed these expressions figuratively, his commentators have elucidated them in different ways: Gérald Antoine, "Max Jacob: Une doctrine littéraire," *FMonde,* 53 (1967), p. 21, interprets "situation" as referring aesthetically to "les lois et les limites du genre"; Blanchet, in his Introduction to the *Défense,* p. 14, chooses a mystical acceptation of the poem situated "à tel ou tel niveau du cosmos divine"; Maurice Pinguet, "L'Ecriture du rêve dans *Le Cornet à dés,*" RLM, Nos. 336-339 (1973), 27, describes the reader — drawn by the poem into the dream state — as "transplanté"; Thau, "Esthetic Reflections," p. 810, n. 5, believes "situation" evokes a "need for obscurity" but concludes that Jacob never clarified the meaning of the term.

espèce de magie qui sépare une œuvre (même picturale ou musicale) de l'amateur, cette espèce de transplantation qui fait que l'œuvre vous met les pieds dans un autre univers." (*Corr.*, I, 132) Through metaphors of displacement in space, Jacob defined artistic pleasure as a profound spiritual event: "Aller en esprit au lieu géographique et surnaturel voulu par un créateur, en revenir c'est une joie de l'esprit et proprement le mouvement qui donne le plaisir artistique." [12] The mystical connotation of the theory of situation may be clearly grasped by comparing Jacob's description of the reader's experience: "On reconnaît qu'une œuvre... est située au petit choc qu'on en reçoit ou encore à la marge qui l'entoure, à l'atmosphère spéciale où elle se meut" (CD, p. 16) with his representation of the mystic's intuition: "Il s'agit d'obtenir le petit choc intérieur qui marque qu'on a compris. C'est plus qu'une adhésion, c'est une descente et comme, chaque fois, une révélation d'une vérité... comme si on passait d'une zone de compréhension à une autre zone." [13] The paradigmatic parallels among his figures of poetic and spiritual transplantation (the shock, the atmosphere or zone, the boundary or margin or passage) expose Jacob's identification of poetic cognition with the knowledge obtained through mystical contemplation.

But there was an important question left unanswered by Jacob's theory of situation. By what means did the poem transplant the reader? In a definition reminiscent of the traditional distinction between skill and genius, he explicitly dissociated "artistic emotion" or "situation" from the stylistic effects of the poem: "Le style ou volonté crée, c'est-à-dire sépare. La situation éloigne, c'est-à-dire excite à l'émotion artistique." (CD, p. 16) For Jacob, style denoted the technical execution and structure of the poem, while situation meant the affectivity of the ensemble; the connection between the whole and its parts remained unspecified: "L'auteur ayant situé son œuvre peut user de tous les charmes; la langue, le rythme, la musicalité et l'esprit." (CD, p. 14) [14] To evoke the irrational, inde-

---

[12] "Les Mots en liberté," MS. 7198-21, located in the Jacques Doucet Collection, Paris.

[13] Lagarde, p. 57.

[14] Henry Decker, in *Pure Poetry, 1925-1930, Theory and Debate in France*, UCPMP, 64 (Berkeley: Univ. of California Press, 1962), p. 19, indicates an analogous dichotomy of techniques and "poetic effect" in the theory of *poésie*

finable affect of the poetic experience, he substituted metaphors of transplantation for logical formulations, thus simulating rather than defining the poem's function: "L'œuvre doit être éloignée *du lecteur*. Elle doit être située dans un espace lointain, entourée d'un monde, vivante dans un au-delà tout en reflétant la terre, portée sur une nuée tout en étant claire. Oui, il faut transplanter." (*Esth.*, p. 31) Here, Jacob's evocation of a far-off space, a world beyond, enveloping the work of art, echoes Mallarmé's idea of a new atmosphere created around the signified object through the isolation of the spoken word: "Le vers qui de plusieurs vocables refait un mot total, neuf, étranger à la langue, et comme incantatoire, achève cet isolement de la parole: niant d'un trait souverain *le hasard* demeuré aux termes malgré l'artifice de leur retrempe alternée en le sens et la sonorité, et vous cause cette surprise de n'avoir ouï jamais tel fragment ordinaire d'élocution, en même temps que la réminiscence de l'objet nommé baigne dans une atmosphère neuve." [15] Both poets regarded the affect produced in the reader as consisting of emotion and revelation, or less precisely, as the emotion of revelation. And yet, Mallarmé, more specifically than Jacob, linked mystical affectivity to verbal processes: *le vers qui de plusieurs vocables refait un mot total, neuf.*

Poetic execution, according to Jacob's theories, involved an analogous transplantation of the poet from one zone of comprehension to another. His *Art poétique* defined inspiration as "le passage d'un monde dans un autre, de la terre au ciel, ou d'un ciel à un autre ciel." (p. 26) This mystical movement initiated the first stage in the creation of the poem, the process of interiorization, or in Jacob's terminology *la vie intérieure*. Interiorization, an irrational activity, preceded the phase of exteriorization, in which the poet consciously chose his techniques or style, defined as "la volonté de s'extérioriser par des moyens choisis." By specifying two levels of poetic execution Jacob concretized his belief in the union of spirit and matter through poetry. For just as in Genesis the spiritual Word of God became incarnate in the universe, the spirit of the poet fused with objects in the words of the poem: "Avant

---

pure of Henri Bremond: "All means of expression, whether rhetorical or 'musical,' fall well within the domain of reason; therefore they cannot be the essence of poetry, which lies beyond the reach of reason."

[15] *Divagations*, p. 256.

d'extérioriser il faut intérioriser: ce passage du fait intérieur au fait extérieur est le verbe." (*Lettres,* p. 248) Meanwhile, the image evoking an intimate verbal bond connecting the two creative stages also tends (like several of Jacob's statements discussed below) to diminish the separation between interiorization and exteriorization. And, once again, the metaphor of the "passage" suggests the equivalence of the poet's, the reader's, and the mystic's experience.

Inspiration, Jacob explained in "La Clef des songes," came to poets and mystics by way of the *Ciel des Images.* Access to this visionary domain could be obtained only after a period of passive waiting, during which time activity of the reflective faculties was suspended: "Les poètes qui pressentent l'inspiration ont, j'imagine, subi l'état d'attente.... C'est une insensibilité! une insensibilité qui s'attend à passer à l'ultrasensibilité.... C'est un abandon de la raison très inconscient avec une adhésion pleine de foi à ce qui pourrait en advenir." ("*Cds,*" p. 580) Yet this condition of detachment was easily induced, not only by fever and drugs, but through dreams, which Jacob hardly distinguished from mystical vision: "Dans les rêves du sommeil, l'esprit n'étant plus attaché à la terre par la sensation, ni à son ciel particulier, flotte dans le ciel le plus voisin de la terre, et il y est le spectateur des clichés les plus voisins." ("*Cds,*" p. 447) Stressing the involuntary nature of the experience, Jacob noted that once the process of inspiration began, it could not be controlled by the inspired subject: "Il voit les clichés du Ciel des Images comme un ruban interminable et même gênant, importun; on ne peut s'en débarrasser: c'est un défilé obligatoire." ("*Cds,*" p. 578) As a correlative to his mystical belief in the *Ciel des Images,* Jacob's theory of poetic inspiration reflected the divergency of thought of his metaphysics: the Platonic idea of eternal forms, the kabbalistic doctrine of inhabited spiritual worlds, the Christian mythology of devils and angels. So that he portrayed spiritual beings as the literal source of artistic genius: "On est inspiré par les anges, les démons et il y a toutes sortes d'anges et de démons. Mais il y a des génies parmi les anges. Quand on a un génie inspirateur, les critiques disent: 'Il a du génie.' " (CJP, p. 27)[16] Aside from his anachronistic, personal belief in

---

[16] This use of a pun on the conventional and concrete senses of "génie" to sum up an idea demonstrates the affinity of Jacob's theoretical and poetic writing.

inspirational angels, Jacob's theory of poetic vision added little but a cosmological framework to the notion of dreams as the material of poetry, an idea actively promulgated by the symbolists.

Yet the revelations of ultimate reality received from the *Ciel des Images* did not in themselves compose the poem. Jacob described a period of meditation in which the images were incorporated into the profoundest level of the poet's existence: "Les idées n'appartiennent pas à l'homme; elles viennent du ciel des images; on se les approprie. Rien de plus triste, de plus pesant que les idées; elles sont toutes de M. Prudhomme et de M. Homais. Elles cessent d'être des idées si vous les ressentez à mort, si vous les ressentez avec passion, avec expérience, si vous *les transformez en sentiments*." (CJP, pp. 20-21) His *Art poétique* metaphorically affirmed the best style to be neither that of the head, nor that of the chest, but rather that of the belly: "Le bon style c'est la spiritualité par en bas. Il y a une pureté du ventre que est rare et excellente." (p. 27) In a letter to Armand Salacrou, he asserted that all stylistic merit was acquired "par le ventre," adding (with a typical play of double meaning) that even the classical style of Madame de Sévigné (writing to her daughter) was "une affaire d'abdomen." [17] Among his later correspondence with Marcel Béalu, there was the recommendation: "Il ne veut pas *le public qui sacre les vrais poètes*, il ne veut pas des petites secousses communes, il veut ce cri propre de tes propres entrailles." (*Lettres*, p. 96) After inspiration, then, must follow the process of "maturation," an emotive assimilation of images or ideas. To Jean Follain, he used the expression "mise en cave," [18] in referring to the subconscious process, which accounted for the originality of poetry: "L'originalité vraie ne peut être que dans la maturation, car ce qui est original c'est le fond de mon moi." (CJP, pp. 18-19) Thus, interiorization involved an inner exploration, a revelation of the poet's self.

Throughout his theoretical writings, Jacob emphasized the value of emotion. Advising young poets, he would reproach them for the inadequacy of their sentiments: "Sentez violemment et vous rendrez naturellement!" (*Corr.*, II, 275) In these contexts the term

---

[17] *Lettres aux Salacrou, août 1923-janvier 1926* (Paris: Gallimard, 1972), p. 12.

[18] Personal communication, July 1966, Paris.

clearly referred to emotion felt during the process of writing: "Ressentir la douleur quand on écrit ce mot, c'est cela la grande Poésie, ressentir l'amour quand on écrit ce mot." (*Lettres*, p. 186) But this was not the only signification the word had in Jacob's poetics. Emotion also meant the response of the reader to the poem: "Propose-toi une intention, un ensemble d'émotions à faire naître." (*Corr.*, II, 188) And the "situation" of the poem, he said, excited "artistic emotion." In an essay entitled "Poésie et pensée abstraite," Paul Valéry recognized an "état poétique" or "inspiration" or "univers poétique" briefly experienced by the poet. It was the function of poetry, he suggested, to recreate this state in the reader: "On reconnaît le poète — ou du moins, chacun reconnaît le sien — à ce simple fait qu'il change le lecteur en 'inspiré.' "[19] Although Jacob did not formulate a direct correlation between the intuitive knowledge gained by the poet through the *vie intérieure* and the mystical cognition transmitted by the poem to the reader, his use of the word "émotion" in both contexts, as well as the paradigm of the revelatory passage of zones, implied an analogy, such as the one made by Valéry.

By representing maturation, the emotive stage of poetic creation, through metaphors of gestation, Jacob conveyed the idea of an involuntary method of writing. As with inspiration, the poet's conscious intervention was excluded from the second phase of the *vie intérieure*: "Une œuvre mûrie trouve d'elle-même son commencement, son milieu et sa fin. Un style mûri prend sa densité comme l'œuf prend de la consistance sous la poule." (CJP, pp. 17-18) In the theory of maturation, the processes of interiorization and exteriorization tended to merge. For words, in an inexplicable manner, emanated automatically from the "descente" of the "œuf," that is, from the reception of inspiration: "Un œuf très grand descend en moi, très profondément, cette descente est accompagnée d'un flux montant d'étincelles lyriques. Ces étincelles sont des mots, des associations de mots." (CJP, p. 57) Jacob's physiological imagery, in the *Conseils*, suggests the definition of poetic execution as the direct recording of sensation: "Autour d'un mot, se coagule une phrase, un vers, une strophe, une idée. Ah! quel beau mode d'extériorisation!" (p. 35) The image of coagulating phrases, then

---

[19] *Œuvres* ("Bibliothèque de la Pléiade"; Paris: Gallimard, 1957), I, 1321.

verses, with its implication of a mode of exteriorization devoid of conscious control, in effect, brings Jacob's poetics close to the Surrealist doctrine of automatic writing.

This concordance is not surprising, since both Jacob and the Surrealists drew their basic assumptions from symbolist theory. The symbolists' ideas on dreams and the Unconscious were adapted in Jacob's theory of the *vie intérieure,* as well as in the Surrealist's oneirism. To late nineteenth-century poets, the Unconscious was a metaphysical entity, existing outside of man, containing universal truths; to Laforgue it represented the "raison explicative, suffisante, unique, intestine, dynamique, adéquate, de l'histoire universelle de la vie."[20] Like the *ciels* of Jacob's cosmology, the metaphysical domain of the Unconscious was immanent and transcendent. So, in the statements of Rémy de Gourmont, the inspired poet's subconscious became the instrument of universal sensations: "Ces hommes surélevés n'atteignent toute leur valeur qu'aux moments où la conscience, devenant subconsciente, ouvre les écluses du cerveau et laisse se précipiter vers le monde les flots rénovés des sensations qu'ils doivent au monde. Ils sont de magnifiques instruments, dont le subconscient seul joue avec génie. Lui aussi, le génie est subconscient."[21] Gourmont's "écluses du cerveau," in touch with the Unconscious universe, became transformed into "déversoirs" in Jacob's *Art poétique,* where the modern poet was urged to "faire frissonner l'inconscient, sonder ses reins, faire servir la poésie à tous les déversoirs pour affirmer qu'on est poète même en dehors du livre à faire." (p. 63) And, as we noted previously, Jacob's notion of interiorization involved not only contact with an external source of inspiration (the *Ciel des Images*), but also an examination of the poet's inner resources: "Le remède est dans une constante *mise au point du "moi." Où suis-je? ma table? mon papier? ma plume?... Tout est LOIN DE MOI, même ce porte-plume que je tiens POURTANT."* (*Esth.,* p. 60) Thus, he echoed the celebrated formula of Rimbaud: "La première étude de l'homme qui veut être poète est sa propre connaissance, entière."[22] For Jacob, as for the symbolists,

---

[20] Cited by Lehmann, p. 115.
[21] *Ibid.,* p. 121.
[22] Arthur Rimbaud, *Œuvres complètes,* ed. Antoine Adam (Paris: Gallimard, 1972), p. 251.

Rimbaud, and, later, the Surrealists, dreams afforded a primary means of obtaining the knowledge of the self and the Unconscious essential to poetic vision.

Symbolist aesthetics, however, failed to explain how the poet utilized unconscious or oneiric material. At precisely what point did he deliberately interfere with the involuntary activity of inspiration? As Herbert Lehmann points out, symbolist theory and poetry allowed for and demonstrated the conscious organization of poetic content.[23] On the other hand, the Surrealists interpreted Rimbaud's appeal for a "long, immense, irraisonné dérèglement de tous les sens,"[24] as well as his poetic method, as a pronouncement for automatism. Jacob's position was ambivalent. His concept of inspiration, demanding an augmentation or diminution of sensation accompanied by "un abandon de la raison très inconscient," adhered to Rimbaud's poetics, as viewed by the Surrealists. As we observed, moreover, in Jacob's *Conseils,* statements on maturation and exteriorization ignored conscious control. Yet, the same collection of aphorisms prescribed the restriction of unconscious impulses: "Le propre du lyrisme est l'inconscience, mais une inconscience surveillée." (CJP, p. 56) Occasionally, Jacob protested still more vehemently against irrational, Surrealistic techniques: "Au point de vue artistique, on avait bien raison d'empêcher les autres de me suivre dans le non-sens, la folie, l'inconscient, le rêve nocturne etc. ... qui n'ont donné que les avortements du surréalisme (celui-ci compliqué de prétentions pseudo-scientifiques, de brutalités et d'orgueils sans fondement.)"[25] On the role of the unconscious in poetic execution, Jacob expressed consistently contradictory opinions.

His reasons for limiting irrational processes differed from the aesthetic motivations of the symbolists. The opposition between automatism and control in Jacob's poetic theories corresponded to the antithesis of the occult and the orthodox in his religious beliefs. For the sake of Christian morality, it was necessary to censor inspiration. Characteristically, Jacob advised a young poet: "Installe un tribunal de toi-même, de tes actes, de tes pensées (surtout de tes pensées). Entre en rapports diplomatiques avec ton ange gardien,

---

[23] *Symbolist Aesthetic,* pp. 88, 117, 121.
[24] *Œuvres complètes,* p. 251.
[25] Cited by Andreu, p. 138. For the personal motives of Jacob's harsh attack, see, my Appendix; see also, Greene, pp. 251-53.

tes voix intérieures et extérieures. Apprends à discerner ce qui vient de toi ou de l'extérieur, les voix des anges et celles des démons (ceux-ci ont des mots grossiers, une voix mécontente, voûtée, coléreuse)." (*Esth.*, p. 26) His *Art poétique* defined Christian art not in respect to devotional themes, but in terms of a style exhibiting moral virtues, such as strength, obedience, order, humility, paucity of wit, sobriety, chastity, and respect. (p. 56) In his correspondence from Saint-Benoît, he indicated the contribution made by the Christian practice of art to the perfection of the pious life. (*Corr.*, II, 93) Although Jacob borrowed Rimbaud's metaphor of the descent into hell (*une saison en enfer*) to represent the poet's exploration of the unconscious, he returned to the symbol its Biblical sense: "J'appelle maturité d'une œuvre sa descente aux enfers. Le Seigneur est descendu aux enfers avant l'Ascension." (CJP, p. 18) If the automatic phase of poetic execution — "maturité d'une œuvre" — comprised communication with infernal forces, then, clearly, the Christian poet had to watch over and modify the dictates of inspiration.

To reconcile his occult poetic theories with his orthodox faith, Jacob not only provided for the censorship of inspiration, but also defined its revelations *a priori*. That is, he assumed the correspondence of the intuitive knowledge gained through poetry and the mystical truths of Christianity, declaring artistic intelligence and Christian intelligence to be synonymous.[26] The poet's goal was established before he began his quest. The *inconnu* of Baudelaire and Rimbaud, the Unconscious of the symbolists, became, for Jacob, the encounter with a specific divinity, mysteriously located within the poet: "Il s'agit d'émotion, et c'est l'essentiel, mais d'une émotion plus profonde que celle du voisin, celle qui vient non de tes sens et de tes nerfs mais de la rencontre enfin! de ton humanité à toi. Or, chose curieuse, cette humanité, perle à dégager, est l'image même de Notre-Seigneur Jésus-Christ.... Mais tu me diras que je te parle à la fois de la descente en toi et de la matière du ciel, quel rapport? Je ne l'explique pas! C'est un fait d'expérience." (*Lettres*, p. 96) Consequently, he linked the talent of the poet with his religious mysticism: "Les exercices mystiques en élévant l'homme élèvent aussi le poète, car tant vaut l'homme tant vaut le poète, et il ne faut pas chercher ailleurs qu'en Dieu un petit supplément

---

[26] Cf. Belaval, p. 122.

d'intelligence. La méditation laïque ne nous fait découvrir que nous-même sans y rien ajouter; mais la grâce de Dieu est vraiment une ajouture au potentiel."[27] From the aesthetic standpoint, however, this theory poses a serious problem, since it places the value of poetry not in the poem, but in the quality of the poet's revelation.

Symbolical exegesis of the Bible, which in Jacob's metaphysics accommodated occult and Christian mysticism, operated analogously in his poetics. Both the *Art poétique* and the *Conseils* (written fifteen years later) represented the creation of the poem through the symbolism of the Sacred Heart. According to Jacob's interpretation, the trajectory of the spear piercing Christ's chest figured the passage of external stimuli into the poet's psyche. In this way, the *Art poétique* explained the religious significance of the poetic process of interiorization: "Le Culte du Sacré-Cœur, le coup de lance ou cinquième plaie est le culte et la marque physique de l'intelligence profonde. Les grandes pensées viennent du cœur, dit un moraliste. Ce qui signifie qu'on ne pense bien que les idées devenues forces de conviction ou sentiment. C'est avec cette intelligence physiologique qu'il faut écrire." (p. 11) Through the metaphor of the Sacred Heart, the stages of inspiration and maturation of the *vie intérieure* were shown to unite spirit and matter in an act of intuitive cognition: "Le Sang et l'eau sortis du Cœur sont l'image de l'union de l'Esprit avec la matière qui est la seule *compréhension* valable. Je pense que vous me comprenez. *Faites descendre*." (CJP, p. 21) The Veronica, too, became an image of poetic execution. Invoking artists and poets in the "Anatomie religieuse," Jacob hypothesized the human face as the symbol of creation, in general, while the Veronica specifically signified artistic creation: "Voyez donc dans cette sainte rencontre de Véronique et du Dieu de Douleur l'Esthétique de la création artistique dans l'ère chrétienne: La Création naît de la rencontre de la douleur et de l'Amour." (MS. 8140-285) As with the Sacred Heart symbolism, the figure suggested the fusion of spirit and matter, of interior and exterior reality, in the poetic process: the poem, like the image of Christ on the Saint's veil, resulted from a spiritual gesture in response to physical suffering.[28]

---

[27] Cited by Emié, p. 179.

[28] Jacob evoked the birth of the poem through the marriage of love and suffering — with a possible allusion to the Veronica in the "voile" of Poetry — in his most frequently quoted religious lyric, "Angoisses et autres":

But by shifting the mystical emphasis from the intuition of occult secrets to knowledge of Christian compassion, these Biblical exegeses implicitly identified poetry with Salvation. And, in fact, Jacob did redefine the emotion at the core of the *vie intérieure* as the experience of suffering: "Si vous n'êtes pas blessé par l'extérieur ou réjoui par l'extérieur, jusqu'à la souffrance, vous n'avez pas la vie intérieure et si vous n'avez pas la vie intérieure, votre poésie est vaine." (CJP, p. 24) At one point, he even proposed the theory of suffering as the ultimate technical solution to poetic execution: "*souffrance comme moyen d'exécution.*" [29] With this proposition, Jacob, in effect, bypassed the symbolists' vague aspirations for mystical cognition to return to the romantic view of poetry as sacramental Communion. Indeed, Jacob's Sacred Heart imagery was not without an affinity to Musset's pelican, symbol of the poet's sacrifice, although the probable model for his representation of the poet as Redemptor was Baudelaire's "Bénédiction":

> —"Soyez béni, mon Dieu, qui donnez la souffrance
> Comme un divin remède à nos impuretés...
> Je sais que vous gardez une place au Poëte
> Dans les rangs bienheureux des saintes Légions." [30]

Yet, in his logical extension of the notion of art as an imitation of the Passion, Jacob confronted a paradox: "Il faut apprendre à souffrir davantage et à se taire. Un vraie poète est tordu sur un bûcher en silence." (*Esth.*, p. 45) For if the poet's task consists of

---

> Sur les remparts d'Edimbourg
> tant de douleur se marie
> ce soir
> avec tant d'amour
> que ton cheval Poésie
> en porte une voile noire. (B, p. 125)

[29] Cited by Lagarde, p. 29.
[30] Charles Baudelaire, *Œuvres complètes* (Paris: Gallimard, 1961), p. 9. Perpetually polarized, Jacob found in his own attraction to the myth of the *poètes maudits*, the point of departure for satirical debunking and ironic self-contempt: "Je veux faire naître dans les autres l'idée de la souffrance des grands artistes, pour qu'on me trouve au moins cette ressemblance avec eux.... Il se mêle bien entendu aussi ici... cet orgueil de la souffrance qui est comme un éloge que nous nous donnons de la finesse de notre nature, qui doit passer pour angélique et supra-humaine." (DT, pp. 151-52)

spiritual perfection achieved through silent meditation, then the poem itself need never be written.

The equation of writing and suffering was antithetical to the definition of art, or style, set forth in the preface to the *Cornet*: "la volonté de s'extérioriser par des moyens choisis." This antithesis, however, constituted only one variant of a fundamental opposition within Jacob's poetics: inspiration versus technique. Throughout his theoretical writings, a dialectical pattern alternated emphasis upon each of these poetic factors. In 1924, he wrote: "Sentez violemment et vous rendrez naturellement! Proportion entre le *senti* et le *rendu*." (*Corr.*, II, 275) And in 1937: "Evidemment l'émotion est l'essentiel de tout art mais le style est aussi 'l'essentiel.'" (*Lettres*, p. 96) By constantly opposing the elements of inspiration and technique, his poetic theories incorporated the predominant aesthetic question of his generation. For with diminishing conformity to the conventions of verse, the traditional attempt to define the nature of poetry had acquired new intensity in the beginning of the twentieth century. Was the essence of poetry located in the affective vision inspiring the poet or the reader, or in the linguistic fabric of the poem? Although Jacob did not participate directly in the contemporary debate on *poésie pure*, which opposed Valéry's emphasis on language to the Abbé Bremond's focus on mystical emotion, the issue preoccupied Jacob. In stressing the ineffable affect of poetry (*situation* or *transplantation*) and the function of inspiration, he followed the symbolist tendency to place poetic evaluation outside the domain of aesthetics. A comparable dilemma arose from Bremond's definition of the mystical essence of *poésie pure*.[31] Within the discussion of pure poetry, moreover, there emerged two antagonistic concepts of technical purity: the precise craftsmanship postulated by Valéry and the direct recording of unconscious sensations promulgated by Dujardin, in defense of Surrealism.[32] Jacob's theories encompassed both these ideas on method in their ambivalent attitude toward automatic devices: "Surveillez l'inconscient, mais laissez-le aller." (*Esth.*, p. 23) In his own terms, Jacob posed crucial questions on the nature, function, and execution of poetry, but his answers invariably equivocated.

---

[31] Decker, p. 110.
[32] *Ibid.*, p. 100.

In focussing alternately on inspiration and technique Jacob reflected his uncertainty concerning the relation of poetry and metaphysics.[33] On occasion, he affirmed the poet to be a mystic: "La lecture des mystiques est le seul conseil d'esthétique. Les grands poètes sont des mystiques sans Dieu (ou avec Dieu) ce que tu appelles la poésie de tonnerre et de source." (*Esth.*, p. 53) As this chapter has demonstrated, many of his poetic theories implied the unity of the two activities, by identifying the experience of the reader and the poet with intuitive knowledge of the divine. Through the Christian connotations of his poetic mysticism, he attributed a sacramental value to art and depicted poetic execution as a religious quest: "Trouvez votre cœur et changez-le en encrier. Le cœur c'est Dieu. Ceci n'est pas un mot littéraire mauvais, c'est une vérité. Dieu n'est pas à l'extérieur mais à l'intérieur de vous. Or vous n'ignorez pas que Dieu est la Perfection. Cherchez donc Dieu en vous-même sans le nommer si vous ne voulez pas être indiscret." (*Esth.*, p. 19) Emotion, God, poetic inspiration, thus, appear united for Jacob. And yet, at times and with varying motivations, he adamantly refuted his own mystical views.

For as an orthodox Catholic, Jacob had to distinguish between poetry and religion.[34] To claim that poetry revealed spiritual realities was unorthodox. Even Jacob's attempts to Christianize his occult theories, equating the poet's suffering with the Passion and interpreting Biblical images as symbols of poetic creation, were heretical, in the manner of his "Anatomie religieuse." A compromise proposed in "La Clef des songes" was the suggestion that poets and mystics experience different degrees of revelation: "Les hommes simplement

---

[33] Again, Jacob's ambivalence accounts for the disagreement among his critics. Blanchet, DT, pp. 16-17, and Marc Le Bot, "Max Jacob, esthéticien?" *Europe*, 36 (avr.-mai 1958), 52, claim Jacob united poetry and mystical faith; Rousselot, p. 146, considers the two activities irrevocably opposed in his life and works; Andreu, p. 106, sees them as separate but compatible interests. Thau, in "Esthetic Reflections," p. 811, insists Jacob differed from other twentieth century theoreticians by refusing to consider poetry as having "a goal other than itself," as "a means of attaining a superior form of knowledge or an intuition of the essence of reality," or as "a source of quasi-mystical experiences for the poet."

[34] His position resembled that of the Abbé Bremond who, as Decker, p. 66, notes, worried "about continued attacks on his orthodoxy because of his supposed equation of poetry and prayer."

contemplatifs étant plus désintéressés le subissent sans doute plus complètement." (p. 580) But this distinction did not, in Jacob's mind, sufficiently reconcile his poetics and his Catholic faith, for he felt the need to emphatically deny the identity of knowledge obtained through poetry and divine Communion: "*Mais la voix de Dieu n'est pas celle de la Poésie. Les génies ne sont pas Dieu bien qu'ils aient été créés par Lui.*" (CJP, p. 15) Carrying the opposition still further, Jacob stated that poetic execution destroyed mystical intuition: "La poésie est un état d'âme à la fois terrestre et supraterrestre accompagné d'un besoin d'extériorisation. L'état mystique est une volupté en Dieu qui ne saurait s'exprimer sans se détruire. L'une est le contraire de l'autre! l'extériorisation détruit la vie intérieure." [35] Yet this assertion came from the poet who also declared: "J'ouvrirai une école de vie intérieure, et j'écrirai sur la porte: école d'art." (CJP, p. 15) Contradictorily, Jacob depicted the poet as a mystic and the act of writing as anathematic to the mystical state.

Jacob's declarations of the incompatibility of poetry and metaphysics were motivated by aesthetic, as well as religious, considerations. If exteriorization could destroy the *vie intérieure* of the poet, his inner life represented a reciprocal danger. While the theory of maturation suggested the direct emanation of the poem from mystical contemplation, that is, the fusion of interiorization and exteriorization, Jacob, at times, maintained the absolute separation of the two stages: "La poésie et la religion s'opposent. Poésie veut dire objectivation et religion veut dire intériorité." [36] Rejecting the romantic valuation of emotion, the cubist movement underscored fabrication, viewed the artist as a craftsman or architect. As a cubist, Jacob declared the emotivity of the mystical state antipodal to the constructive activity of writing:

> Je ne crois pas qu'il y ait aucune similitude entre la religion, la Voyance et la Poésie. La Poésie est une *objectivation,* le martèlement d'un rythme. La religion est une fièvre intérieure qui, exprimée, ne donne que le contraire de la poésie: des balbutiements, des exclamations ou la Symbolique compliquée de Saint Jean de la Croix. Quoi de

---

[35] Cited by Emié, p. 179.
[36] Cited by Andreu, p. 104.

plus comique qu'un orateur qui sent. L'Orateur magicien qui ensorcelle et semble ému ne sent peut-être rien. Etre religieux, c'est vivre intérieurement. Etre poète, c'est *ruisseler*, c'est-à-dire sentir moins qu'on ne dit.[37]

In such statements, his dilemma was not that poetry would dissipate mystical ecstasy or usurp the spiritual prerogatives of religion, but that mystical inspiration would result in a sentimental style.

If Jacob's poetic theories linked poetry and prayer, they also polarized art and faith. Thus, the contradictions informing his theoretical writings cannot be reduced to a simple antithesis between aesthetics and ethics.[38] For analogous divisions marked Jacob's thinking on metaphysics and on poetry. While his mystical theories of situation, inspiration, and maturation corresponded to his occult beliefs and Christian mysticism, his limitation of poetic cognition and unconscious processes responded to the demands of his Catholic orthodoxy.

Consistency, however, is not a prerequisite for poetry, nor is contradiction a sign of artistic failure. In the poetics practiced by Jacob, he effectively balanced the antitheses which undermined his theoretical affirmations. The immeasurable affect of mystical inspiration was complemented by technical skill. The contrariety of conscious and unconscious modes of writing, unresolved in theory, created expressive stylistic contrasts in his poems. And, through a counterpoint of oneirism and lyrical confession, Jacob dramatically transposed the conflict of the occult and the orthodox. Opposition, contradiction, discordancy were the characteristic elements of his poetry. His poetic theory most consistently applicable to his own writing was, perhaps, a unique and brief allusion to the concept of aesthetic doubt: "Il faut *ballotter* le spectateur: l'émotion esthétique est le doute. Le doute s'obtiendra par l'accouplement de ce qui est incompatible... par l'accord des langages différents.... Le doute voilà l'art." (*Corr.*, I, 31)[39] For the movement of antithesis —

---

[37] Cited by Emié, p. 177.

[38] This was Rousselot's, p. 146, view of the problem: "Peut-on être un poète de plein exercice, c'est-à-dire quelqu'un qui ajoute une réalité au '*patrimoine cosmique*' en même temps qu'un catholique orthodoxe? Tel est le dilemme."

[39] This principle of linking opposites, in effect, sums up the characteristic tendency of modern poetry since Rimbaud. Poets have experimented with the

l'accouplement de ce qui est incompatible — impelled Jacob's metaphysics, his poetics, and his poetry.

---

method in essentially two ways: by following the approach either of Reverdy, who ultimately sought the true rapport of distant realities, or of Breton, who emphasized the gratuitous quality of the associations. Cf. M. Carrouges, *André Breton et les données fondamentales du surréalisme,* 3rd edition (Paris: Gallimard, 1950), pp. 120-21.

Je ne saurais trop insister sur ce point, mon cher ami, que tout le sel du livre est dans le contraste qui existe entre le burlesque et le mystique, et c'est là l'essentiel.

Max Jacob, *Correspondance*

Chapter III

THE EVOLUTION AND THE DIALECTIC OF
POETIC STYLE

In 1910, a few months after the revelation in the Rue Ravignan and before Max Jacob published his first collection of poems, he announced the three major tendencies of his poetic style. Writing to Henry Kahnweiler, the art dealer patron of cubist painters and poets, Jacob described the divergent modes of his poetry as burlesque, confessional, and enigmatic:

> J'ai mis sur pied trois volumes de poèmes qui vous agréeront peut-être un jour. Le premier s'appelle "Poèmes burlesques", il contient des parodies, des inventions burlesques, des jeux de musique verbale, des chansons, et obtiendra le rire qu'il désire faire naître. Le second s'appelle "Poèmes d'Orient et de Bretagne"; il est plein d'intimité et de confessions quotidiennes. Son charme est dans sa grâce et sa tristesse; c'est le côté verlainien du pauvre Lélian que je suis. Le tout bien imprévu, comme de juste. Le troisième s'appelle "Le Livre des Enigmes". C'est une série de poèmes persans très colorés qui sont faits pour faire croire à mon génie. (Corr., I, 43) [1]

---

[1] In an unpublished letter to Marguerite Mespoulet, cited by Annette Thau, in *Poetry and Antipoetry: A Study of Selected Aspects of Max Jacob's Poetic Style,* North Carolina Studies in the Romance Languages, Essays, No. 5 (Chapel Hill: U.N.C. Dept. of Romance Languages, 1976), p. 15, Jacob used another terminology to represent his three stylistic tendencies: "humour, amour, inconscience." These terms would appear to correspond to the modes of burlesque, confession, and enigma, respectively. "Enigma" is a vague expression, but in the context of the letter to Kahnweiler, it apparently refers to devices evoking visionary or oneiric imagery.

The allusion to Paul Verlaine in this context was significant. In the last of his essays on the *poètes maudits* (signed with the anagrammatic pseudonym *le pauvre Lélian*), Verlaine had defended the appearance of disunity in his poetry on psychological grounds. He explained that his poems were meant to reflect both the sensuous and the mystical, the pious and the intellectual aspects of his personality. Deliberately, then, Verlaine would develop two poetic motifs "simultanément": the one communicating feelings of "délectation" toward temptation and sin, the other projecting sentiments of "remords." [2]

Jacob's justification of the diversity of his own style followed the example of Verlaine by associating spiritual attitudes with stylistic effects. In place of Verlaine's notion of simultaneity, however, Jacob hypothesized an evolution in his poetic method. His first novel, *Saint Matorel* (1911), narrated — on the fantastical and parodic level — an account of the religious conversion of his fictional surrogate, Victor Matorel. A year later, the *Œuvres burlesques et mystiques de Frère Matorel mort au couvent,* Jacob's second collection of poems, were presented as the pseudo-productions of the fictitious Matorel. In its prospectus, Jacob elaborated the myth of Matorel's (i.e., of his own) poetic evolution. As in the letter to Kahnweiler, the dominant elements of his poetry were identified as burlesque ("Mark Twain"), enigmatic ("poèmes obscurs"), and confessional ("lamartinien"). But this time, he represented them hierarchically, as stages in the parallel evolution of poetry and faith: "Les plus anciens poèmes, ceux de l'époque où nous avons connu Matorel employé, sont pleins de curieuses recherches de rimes et rythmes, d'anecdotes qui semblent d'un Mark Twain poète et mystérieux; puis le ton s'élargit, au fur et à mesure que la Vérité vient à lui, les poèmes deviennent obscurs, jusqu'au jour que la grâce éclate, alors c'est comme une trouée de lumière: Matorel se révèle lamartinien; certes le style y perd mais le sentiment y gagne." (*Corr.,* I, 66-67)

Here the difference between the apologies of Jacob and Verlaine becomes clear. By underscoring the preference of Matorel's religious

---

[2] Paul Verlaine, *Œuvres complètes* (Paris: Club des Librairies de France, 1959), I, 887. The essay first appeared in the review *La Vogue* (June 1886) and then in *Les poètes maudits* (1888).

poetry for sentiment rather than style, Jacob signaled his ironic intention. In retrospect, even his earlier allusion to *le pauvre Lélian* might be considered tongue-in-cheek, especially since the narrator of Saint Matorel, on several occasions, depreciates both Verlaine and religious motifs: "Remarquez comment les Idées 'Hôpital, Couvent, Prison, Remords, Paul Verlaine,' s'embrouillent et cohabitent facilement chez ce malheureux, sans doute petit-fils de tuberculeux ou d'avarié." (SM, n.pag.) And, in a similar manner, the pseudo-editor of the *Œuvres burlesques et mystiques* called attention to the absence of cohesion and to the weak rhymes of its purportedly confessional or "Lamartinian" poems. (OBM, n.pag.)[3] These ironic overtones to the myth of Matorel/Jacob's poetic evolution corresponded to the aesthetic doubts entertained by Jacob during the period of his conversion. The fear that *le mauvais style* was an inevitable by-product of religious inspiration preoccupied him as he prepared to adopt the Catholic faith: "Mon Dieu, cher ami, quel trouble me prend devant tout cela! il me vient parfois tant de larmes et je me sens si catholique déjà que le mauvais style m'arrive avec elles." (*Corr.*, I, 105)

It is not surprising, then, that Jacob's earliest poems contained few signs of *confessions quotidiennes,* while they displayed the full range of his *inventions burlesques* and *Enigmes*. Although the poetry of *La Côte* (1911) did include affective statements, by parodying Breton folk lyrics, it established an ironic distance between the poet (or the reader) and the speakers of its emotive monologues.[4] The verse poems of the *Œuvres burlesques et mystiques* exemplified the "jeux de musique verbale" and "chansons," whose effects, as Jacob noted in the letter to Kahnweiler, were primarily humorous. Like the following experimentation with interversion of phonemes, this poetry focussed on the dichotomy of the sound and the sense of words:

---

[3] These comments do not appear in the revised edition published by Gallimard in 1936.

[4] In spite of Jacob's retrospective attempts to dissociate this work from the "objective" style of the *Cornet* — cf. Max Jacob *Corr.*, II, 327; Max Jacob, *Lettres à un ami* (Paris: Editions Vineta, 1951), p. 37 — and the insistence of some critics on his debt to the inspiration of Breton folklore, the predominance of the parodic orientation in *La Côte* has been demonstrated by Jean de Palacio, in "Un Précurseur inattendu de Max Jacob: Lord Byron," *Revue de littérature comparée,* 45ᵉ ann., No. 2 (avr.-juin 1971), 190-94.

> Variation d'une formule
> La bourse houe! avis!
> La bourse ou la vie!
> Là bout sous la vie
> (Glas! boue!) sourd, l'ami
> Glabre, ours sous l'habit. (SM/OBM, p. 229)

The predominant effects of the prose poems of the same volume were ambiguity and obscurity, or to use Jacob's term, enigma. Anecdotes whose events lack causal connection, tableaux suggesting latent symbolic meanings, mysterious metamorphoses of objects and persons, these poetic devices have often been compared to the construction of the dream-work, the *écriture du rêve,* in which the poet assumes all the fantasized parts: [5]

> Et les acacias laissaient pleuvoir leurs grappes! Dans vos jeux, adolescentes australiennes — oh! les verts caoutchoucs d'une cour de collège! — saute une japonaise. Pourtant le frère yankee d'une pégadogue l'aimait. O amours du haut d'une fenêtre! le père de Tokio, ancien pirate, hait la pédagogie dans son palais.
>
> Là-dessus planait le vol d'un aigle ou ange. Et là-bas dans les ports s'en allaient des bateaux vers les minerais d'émeraudes et les chevaux nains. La japonaise avait des lunettes et les acacias laissaient pleuvoir leurs grappes. (SM/OBM, p. 233)

To decipher the enigmas or visions of the *Œuvres burlesques et mystiques* was the task of the reader, for Jacob provided no explicit indications of the poem's hidden meaning. Nor did the metalinguistic commentaries of the pseudo-editor offer reliable guidelines, since his rhetoric parodically exaggerated critical style and, thereby, undermined his own assertions: "De son excursion dans la littérature moderne, Matorel n'a-t-il rapporté qu'un nom et qu'une œuvre: le nom et l'œuvre d'Arthur Rimbaud? Nous ne pouvons le voir avec certitude. Où commence, où finit l'ironie chez cet employé-poète?" (SM/OBM, p. 238) Allusions to religious sentiments occur rarely in this collection; and when emotive statements do appear, it is difficult to decide whether they should be

---

[5] Cf. Belaval, pp. 85-86; Pinguet, "L'Ecriture du rêve," pp. 13-52; Thau, *Poetry and Antipoetry,* pp. 82-83.

taken at face value or read ironically. Yet Plantier, pp. 32-36, claims these early works, in fact, marked Jacob's spiritual evolution from kabbalism to Catholicism, from the quest for visionary knowledge to the desire for personal salvation.[6] However, even if we were to accept his interpretation of the irony of the *Œuvres burlesques et mystiques* and of *Saint Matorel* as a smoke screen for the confessions of faith Jacob hesitated to signify overtly, it would be more accurate to view the works as transpositions of an unresolved conflict than as signs of its conclusion.

Indeed, the conception of the prose poem elaborated in the Preface to the *Cornet à dés* (1917) provided a direct contradiction to the myth of Matorel/Jacob's evolution toward confessional lyricism. Like the cubist painting, the poem was to be considered a constructed object, whose aesthetic appeal Jacob differentiated from the sensory as well as the sentimental: "L'émotion artistique n'est ni un acte sensoriel, ni un acte sentimental; sans cela, la nature suffirait à nous la donner." (p. 15) The *Cornet,* in practice, confirmed the theory of its Preface. Thus Oxenhandler, p. 226, observed of its method: "It is a style that has attained the extreme limit of the personal by abolishing all traces of the personality." This is not to say that Jacob's early prose poems entirely lacked lyrical expressivity, but rather that they avoided reference to the emotive state of the poetic speaker. The latter had to be inferred from the interrelation of textual elements. Dominated by the tendency toward absurd humor and enigma, the *Cornet*'s texts manifested anxiety without necessarily assigning to the sentiment a specific subject, a logical cause, or even a precise name. Jacob's oneiric images, as Belaval, p. 85, was the first to point out, evoked prereflexive apprehensions: "L'angoisse la plus solitaire, dans un monde où les choses se déconsistent, cessent d'être pour elle-mêmes et forment un mur d'inquiétude qu'on ne parvient pas à franchir."

---

[6] On the other hand, Neal Oxenhandler, "Max Jacob and *Les Feux de Paris,*" 35 (1964) UCPMP, 228-29, situates the evolution toward orthodoxy between 1924 and 1926, but does not specify the date or the specific nature of the consequent changes in poetic style: "In Max's later years, the integrity of man and artist became ever more interdependent; the poet's imagination, by the very fact that the poet accepted its finitude, was found to contain infinity under the species of grace. There is a gentleness in the older Max, not to be confused with a decline in power, for Max retained his amazing energy and vigor to the end."

After the *Cornet*'s brilliant formulation and illustration of the theory of the poem object, the dedication of Jacob's next work incites surprise. The *Défense de Tartufe* (1919) opens with a return to the idea of the poet's parallel stylistic and spiritual progression: "Les étapes de ce livre, marquées par des œuvres poétiques, peut-être, conduisent l'auteur au catholicisme, du libertinage, dont le mysticisme ne l'avait pas guéri, à la première Révélation." (p. 73) Is the reader to take this declaration seriously? Anyone familiar with the Matorel myth would incline toward scepticism. Certainly, Jacob encouraged doubt by placing the word "peut-être" in an ambivalent position, so that it implies either the literary inadequacy of the poems or the doubtfulness of the author's conversion. The title, of course, provokes questions. Is the text a defense of Molière's character? Or does it invent a new personage named Tartufe? [7] Or is "Tartufe" simply an epithet for Jacob himself? Whatever the case, the "defense" of a hypocrite appears problematic.

Baroquely subtitled, *Extases, remords, visions, prières, poèmes et méditations d'un Juif converti*, the *Défense de Tartufe* is a hybrid work defying classification by genre, and creating a tension between fiction and autobiography. It claims to sketch the life of the author Tartufe (alternately called "le poète," "le Juif converti," "le libertin") in brief narrative prologues to each of its four sections, in fragments of a journal, in prose self-examinations, and in religious meditations. Although the events of this narration and of Jacob's own existence are similar, several obvious discrepancies weaken the status of the *Défense* as confession. On the one hand, the poetry purportedly reflects the four chronological stages of the poet's spiritual evolution: (1) before his revelation; (2) during and immediately after his revelation; (3) between his revelation and his retreat from society; (4) after his retreat. But an examination of the manuscripts shows that the order of the poems represents an arrangement decided at the time of publication, not in accord with

---

[7] The question is not resolved by the difference between Jacob's spelling of "Tartufe" (with one *f*) and Molière's spelling of "Tartuffe" (with double *ff*), for Littré gives the orthograph "Tartufe" (with one *f*) for the name of Molière's personage, as well as for the second meaning cited: "(avec un *t* miniscule) faux dévot, hypocrite, coquin se servant du manteau de la religion." Blanchet (DT, p. 64) notes that Jacob did not adopt the orthograph with one *f* until the second proofs.

the chronology of composition.[8] Moreover, the prologue of the last part states: "Le poète, ayant abandonné le monde pour le faire du péché, trouve dans le catholicisme ce qu'il ne trouvait pas dans le mysticisme: la paix." (p. 181) This point contradicts circumstances in Jacob's life, since he had not yet retired from Paris to Saint Benoît.

Viewed in the perspective of Jacob's total writing and experiences, however, the *Défense* becomes significant both as a poetic manifesto and as a confession. In spite of factual inaccuracies, its journal, self-examinations, and meditations expressed feelings and preoccupations common to Jacob's personal correspondence of the period. For example, the repeated insistence, through direct confessions, on the conflict between literature and the practice of religion: "Obéir, moi! quand j'ai passé ma vie à désobéir à tous et à tout: je ne puis obéir qu'à mon goût sinon qu'à mes goûts. Me laissera-t-on faire l'art que je veux?" (DT, p. 117) Between occult and orthodox doctrines: "J'ai eu des doutes sur la vérité vivante de la vie du Christ telle que l'Evangile l'enseigne; les pratiques de l'occultisme m'avaient habitué à n'y voir que des symboles." (DT, p. 159) Between temptation and remorse: "Car je n'ai jamais pu distinguer la part de pureté et celle d'impureté qui se mêlaient dans mes affections.... Pour plaire, je me suis vu presque à renier ma religion!" (DT, p. 164) Between the fear of death and hope for salvation: "Quand mourrai-je? Où? Comment? Sera-ce à l'hôpital? dans cette chambre? au couvent? dans un appartement somptueux? à terre dans la rue? Dans ma famille? aurai-je persévéré dans la foi? aurai-je fait des progrès vers la perfection? ou me serai-je endurci dans le mal! serai-je en état de grâce?" (DT, p. 227) These, in effect, were the lyrical motifs to predominate in Jacob's subsequent religious poetry.

But they operated first in the poetry of the *Défense,* where Jacob's confessional tendency (announced nine years before) finally received emphasis, along with accompanying religious themes. So that the *Défense de Tartufe,* as its dedicatory remarks claimed, manifested an evolution of his poetic method. The subtitles of its

---

[8] For example, Blanchet, DT, p. 255, indicates that the poem "Pas encore" was written in 1912 in Quimper. It was placed, however, in the third part of the *Défense,* supposedly containing texts composed after the poet's baptism.

four parts — "L'Antithèse," "La révélation," "La décadence ou mystique et pécheur," "La vie dévote" — suggest a dialectic in which the antithesis of scepticism and faith produces a spiritual conflict resulting in the new life of the penitent Christian. And, to a certain extent, this process was stylistically actualized: the first group of poems relied on burlesque techniques; the second section created primarily visionary effects; the third contrasted the three major tendencies of Jacob's style; and the last group depended on the confessional mode. Yet the significant factor in terms of Jacob's stylistic evolution was not the simulated progress towards devotional lyricism, but the juxtaposition (in the *Défense* as a whole and in its individual texts) of incongruous effects. For the early poetic devices by no means dwindled away in the later poems. On the contrary, a consistent pattern of stylistic contrasts, obtained, as Jacob had prescribed, "par l'accouplement de ce qui est incompatible," determined the structure of his religious poetry.

A brief analysis of several prose poems of the *Défense* will demonstrate the contrast of confessional and enigmatic effects. Jacob's multifold devices for expanding the connotations of ordinary language, which produced an atmosphere of mystery in the *Œuvres burlesques et mystiques* and the *Cornet,* continued to function in the *Défense*. But, while his earlier texts heightened ambiguity by avoiding explanations of personal symbolism, his later prose poems provided clues to interpretation. Titles, parenthetical expressions, appositives, interjections, exclamations, interrogations typically served as indicators of the emotive meaning of the text. The pointedly entitled poem, "Péché dans la recherche de la vertu," for instance, combines oneirism and confession by associating the visually evocative phrase "réapparition de la grand'mère" with a sense of guilt, through the appositive "mémoire d'un mal fidèle," and by identifying the reference to "bas blancs rayés en travers" as a mystical sign of moral import, through the parenthetical expression: "(signe de démonialité)." These narratorial interferences reduce polyvalence, attaching personal denotations to the accumulation of impersonally expressive signifiers:

> Réapparition de la grand'mère! mémoire d'un mal fidèle. Une voix creuse et salée du monde invisible de l'oreille: "Bonsoir!" Bas blancs rayés en travers (signe de démonialité) sur le tapis rouge. Je fuis à travers les fleurs aussi

> innombrables que des herbes et, quand je veux cueillir le jasmin sauvage, c'est un arbre que je secoue et il est mort. Que faire? mon père, secourez-moi! (DT, p. 146)

In respect to aesthetics, such rhetorical devices suggest the deliberate activity of the poet, while the contrasting oneiric techniques give the impression of verbal association without reflective ordering. The poem thus transposes the antithesis noted earlier in Jacob's poetic theories: the opposition of automatic or unconscious writing to conscious composition.

While the sense of mystery did not entirely disappear from the *Defense*'s prose poems, it was attenuated by the intercalation of emotive statements linking ambiguously suggestive signifiers to precise confessional motifs. The closing interrogative and exclamation of "Péché dans la recherche de la vertu," for example, disclose the affective reaction of the poetic speaker to the preceding visionary images: "Que faire? mon père, secourez-moi!" The pattern reappears in three poems of the section entitled "Révélation." In "Entrevue," visual evocations succeed one another in a lexically incongruous arrangement that commentators, according to their orientation, might label "oneiric," "cubist," or "apocalyptic."[9] But the orientation of the poem's last line is emotive:

> Un rayon d'or s'enroule et forme une couronne. Il y a du monde autour de mon lit, mais personne ne le verra que moi. Le cheval domine la mer, étoffe froissée. Sur la mer, une femme s'élève auréolée et un poète au piano demande à Dieu de l'inspirer. Des incendies s'allument au loin. Que suis-je, qu'un esclave à genoux, un esclave dont je ne reconnais pas le regard? (DT, p. 104)

Exhibiting a homologous structure, the prose poems entitled "Signification" and "Exhortation" conclude, respectively, with an interrogation: "Vaut-il mieux comprendre que prier, ou prier que comprendre?" (p. 105) and with an interrogative followed by a predicate adjective focussing on a (deprecatory) attribute of the lyrical I: "Quand j'aurai le Saint-Esprit, me donnera-t-il le don des langues? L'Ange est furieux de me voir si bête." (p. 106) In each

---

[9] E.g., Thau, Kamber, Blanchet, respectively.

instance, the final question evokes a Christian framework, not only thematically but stylistically as well, for the rhetoric of devotional literature traditionally employed interrogation to emphasize the dramatic participation of the speaker in the Biblical events contemplated.[10]

In the preceding examples, the opposition of enigmatic and confessional contexts reflected semantic complementarity, for the latter tended to interpret the former. But contrasting stylistic effects may equally serve the function of reinforcing thematic contradictions. The opening verse of the *Défense*'s "La Messe du visionnaire" seems to exhort the poetic speaker: "Ne souris plus, si c'est la fin du monde!" (DT, p. 138) There follows an abrupt break with the emotive context: the description of a vision, presumedly sent by Christ from the Cross. The disparate elements of this symbolically suggestive, yet impenetrable, tableau include a winged cask, a blond Gauloise, a Virgin, clouds and halos, helmeted soldiers, a cherubin with an ocellated insect's wing, a chandelier. This last unexpected detail provokes the return to the confessional mode, as the lyrical I interrupts the impersonal enumeration to express curiosity, then doubt, and finally remorse:

> Ange gardien, pourquoi ce chandelier?
> Si c'est d'amour que tu me veux lier,
> Ne me fais pas curieux d'hyperespace;
> Je ne veux pas d'autre don que la grâce!

Humorous, surreal visions become a source of anxiety for the poetic speaker, who rejects them as incompatible with personal salvation: "Mais le plaisir me détourne de Dieu. / Cœur de croyant n'a pas besoin des yeux." The lyrical I resists oneirism; and the poem, through stylistic antithesis, transposes the poet's conflicting desires for mystical knowledge and for Christian redemption.

It was not a question in the *Défense*'s contrasts of the negation of one tendency by another, nor of synthesis, for Jacob's poetic method relied upon the maintenance of tension. Just as, in his

---

[10] See Terence C. Cave, *Devotional Poetry in France c. 1570-1613* (Cambridge, Eng.: Cambridge Univ. Press, 1969), p. 33. An analogous function characterizes the interrogative in Raymond Lull's *Le Livre de l'ami et de l'aimé*, the mystical dialogues translated into French by Jacob.

religious experience, sin generated remorse and remorse entailed self-deprecation, so in his poetry the visionary and the burlesque induced confession and confession, in turn, became the parody of confession. If we were to ignore the telling title of the prose poem "Dieu nous a abandonnés" and neglect the epigraph: "Pécher, pécher, se repêcher" with the signature "Max Jacob," we would undoubtedly interpret the text as black humor in the absurd mode. (DT, p. 113) An anecdote resembling a dream, an orgy in a studio of Montparnasse interrupted by the entry of a priest and a religious procession, a visitor announcing himself as "le bon Dieu," in reality, "le commissaire de police, un vilain moustachu avec sa ceinture." The terrestrial forces of law and order, ironically, become confused with the celestial Lord and his earthly representatives. Who can take seriously a God metamorphosed into a police commissioner? Yet, on the other hand, we do not forget the title, which at the outset establishes the confessional context, allowing us to read the poem as a metaphor of the quest for spiritual amelioration: the mistaken identities, reminiscent of detective novels, represent the difficulty of finding God in contemporary society; the agitation produced by the surprising disturbance of the orgy — "Tout le monde est plein d'effroi!" — corresponds to the sinner's consciousness of evil. The opposition of burlesque oneirism and lyrical confession dramatizes the thematic conflict of sin and remorse, forecast and summed up, on the phonetic level, in the epigraph.

Similarly, a thematic antithesis of faith and skepticism emanates from the stylistic structure of "Le Christ au cinématographe," where parodic effects counterpoint a predominantly confessional orientation. The verse poem evokes a dramatic situation autobiographically inspired by Jacob's second revelation: the poet in a movie house, a cloak-and-dagger film, the arrival of a mysterious heavenly spirit, the apparition of a Christ-like figure on the screen. A logical sequence of affective statements move the lyrical I from an attitude of supplication:

> Dryade du Gibet, descends comme hier au soir
> Dans la stalle du Ciné, lorsque tu vins t'asseoir
> Près de moi. Ta main! mets ta main sur la mienne
> Et ta chaleur humaine et ta divine haleine! (DT, p. 127)

Through a sense of ecstatic wonder: "A moi, cette faveur! pourquoi cette venue?" To a stance of humility and gratitude: "Si tu connais mes fautes et toutes mes faiblesses / Qu'y a-t-il donc en moi, mon Dieu, qui t'intéresse?" Yet to consider only these emotive elements falsifies the poetic experience; we must pay attention to the ironic overtones. The theme of the presence of the Holy Spirit within commonplace settings (such as a movie house) in a sense connotes the intensity of the speaker's primitive mysticism: "Sentir en soi son Dieu, l'écouter, lui parler, / Qu'on soit dans un théâtre, dans la rue, au café." But the motif becomes comically absurd, when the lyrical I insists unnecessarily upon exact detail: "C'était aux places à quatre-vingt-quinze-centimes." In several instances, moreover, the emphatic protestation of the speaker undercuts his own self-defense. Addressing imaginary interlocutors, his rapid change of tone appears histrionic. Grumbling about the incredulity of his readers: "—On me traite de fou! oui! j'entends le lecteur." Indignantly returning their imagined invectives: "Fous vous-mêmes si la vérité vous fait rire." Self-righteously predicting and parrying his listener's accusations: "—Non! je n'étais pas gris, je suis un homme sobre." Or, flippantly turning aside the admonishments of his confesseur:

>"Vous allez donc alors au Cinématographe,
>Me dit un confesseur, la mine confondue.
>—Eh! mon père! le Seigneur n'y est-il pas venu?"

This is the voice of the clown at the altar, of the penitent whose affirmations of faith alternate with their own self-parody. In "Le Christ au cinématographe" the immediate juxtaposition of emotive and burlesque contexts produces comic surprise, but in the wider context of the poem the antithesis concretizes the disquietude of a contradictory spiritual experience.

One of the most interesting aspects of Jacob's religious poetry, equally exhibited in the *Défense,* was its self-consciousness. "La Messe du démoniaque" illustrates the deliberate attention drawn to the pattern of stylistic contrasts within the text. As the title implies, the poem parodies the liturgy, recalling the model of the mass through corrupt Latin incantations and syntactical constructions imitative of hymns. As in the mass, several voices alternate. One is that of a demoniacal choir, whose disruptive use of word-

THE EVOLUTION AND THE DIALECTIC OF POETIC STYLE 79

play disarticulates the liturgical phrase *Misericordia anima mea* and recombines its phonemes to form the words "mama" and "maria." This juxtaposition generates an association based on sense articulated in the expression "la grosse ma ... Maria." From this humorous play on sounds and significations, there then emerges a sacrilegious tableau in the visionary mode. Propelled by suggestive word-play, the vision (depicting a pregnant Virgin) semantically contradicts the doctrine of the Immaculate Conception:

> Il fait nuit, plutôt nuit, plutôt crasse, ploutocratie.
> Notre Seigneur se gonfle, se dégonfle: il voudrait sortir.
> La dernière statue de Marie — celle de gauche,
> S'attache, se détache — ô pardonnez-moi, pardon,
>   est-ce un rêve?
> —S'attache un groin ... comme les autres,
> Comme toutes les autres, d'ailleurs. (DT, p. 167)

Intercalated within the burlesque/oneiric chant of the demonic choir, the emotive statements of the lyrical I refer to the penitent's sense of innocence, his remorse, his fear of damnation. In a movement analogous to the censorship of the unconscious by the *cogito*, a sequence of metalinguistic warnings opposes the apparently uncontrolled flow of the text:

> Oh! je vous en prie ...
> (Je ne permettrai pas que vous écriviez une chose pareille
> Vous serez damné pour avoir osé chose pareille).

The censor's intervention, however, does not arrest the blasphemy. In the last lines of the poem, a stylistic contrast figures the spiritual dilemma of the lyrical I: an emotive plea for assistance is followed by an attempt to decipher the hidden meaning of Christian concepts, of the soul and the mass. But this orphic exercise leads to confusion mirrored in the disintegration of language itself, as the lines move from rational interrogation to non-sensical paronomasia, to sentence fragmentation, to the enunciation of stuttered, isolated syllables:

> Que faire? c'est-à-dire
> Ce que peut bien signifier le l'âme, la messe, l'ânesse
> En dehors de ... de la ... de ...

As with many of Jacob's superficially incoherent texts, the formal structure of "La Messe du démoniaque" affords the key to interpretation. The final breakdown of communicability conveys the failure of the lyrical I to subordinate irrational, irreverent impulses. The poetic speaker's metalinguistic allusions oppose emotive confession associated with the motifs of Christian humility and repentance to automatic writing connected with the themes of sensuality and skepticism. Thus, the text consciously draws a parallel between stylistic and spiritual disorder.

The project of uniting disparate poetic tendencies through contrast was the common design of the poetry written by Jacob after the *Défense de Tartufe*. Although not yet developed in the *Laboratoire central* (1921), where verbal experimentation predominated, the contrastive method prevailed in the *Visions infernales* (1924), in *Les Pénitents en maillots roses* (1925), in *Fond de l'eau* (1927), *Sacrifice impérial* (1929), *Rivages* (1934), and in the posthumous collections, *Derniers poèmes* (1945) and *L'Homme de cristal* (1948).[11] Yet the pattern of stylistic oppositions did not serve a monolithic function in these poems. Contrasts between burlesque, enigmatic, and confessional contexts intensified expressiveness by creating a variety of effects. As we observed in several pieces of the *Défense,* a frequent result was the reinforcement of thematic contradictions, such as the antitheses of temptation and penitence, of doubt and faith, of occultism and orthodoxy. Or, stylistic polarization might emphasize semantic complementarity, as in the instance of interpretative emotive statements and of oneiric signifiers serving as an objective correlative to lyrical motifs. The general function, however, of the formal antithetical structure of Jacob's religious poetry was to recreate the dramatic atmosphere of his spiritual life.

The method of the *Visions infernales* derived directly from the prose poems of the *Défense,* in which confessional devices deciphered the mystical significance of enigmatically related signs. As

---

[11] Most of the pieces included in *Le Laboratoire central* were written before the publication of the *Défense.* I have omitted discussion of the *Poèmes de Morven le Gaëlique* — first published in the review *La Ligne de Cœur* (1926-31) — and later in a posthumous volume (1953) and of *Ballades* (1938), because of the predominance of parody in the former and the absence of religious themes in the latter collection.

THE EVOLUTION AND THE DIALECTIC OF POETIC STYLE 81

Jacob stated, his purpose was to situate the images of the *Cornet* in a Christian moral order: "Les *Visions infernales,* Cornet à Dés chrétien, est plutôt effroyable que bluette." (*Corr.,* II, 22) In the similarities and differences of these two volumes of prose poems lies the explication of Jacob's poetic evolution. For the *Visions infernales* retained the effects of anguish and disconcerting humor of the earlier dream writing in order to evoke the decor of hell. To convey a sense of menacing mystery, for example, the poem "Voir sa mort dans sa vie" does not depend on traditional infernal symbolism, but instead displaces commonplace objects and events. How does the poetic speaker move instantaneously from a staircase to a bed to a ravine to a revolving train platform? Why does a river run through the railroad station? These incongruities suddenly transforming everyday reality make the reader uneasy:

> J'ai monté la ligne droite de l'escalier brillant: en haut l'image horrible du démon m'attendait. Sous les rideaux du lit l'image horrible m'attendait: le démon!
>
> J'ai escaladé la pente du ravin: elle est pleine de fleurs et le trottoir du débarcadère tourne autour du fleuve, personne qu'un employé des gares: mais dans son regard j'ai lu qu'il n'était là que pour signifier ce qu'il représente: le démon!
>
> Les trains se croisent! les trains sont vides! vide est la campagne autour de la gare. Mais un voyageur descend qui m'inspecte avec le plus terrible sourire et dans son sourire j'ai lu qu'il n'était là que pour signifier ce qu'il représente: le démon. (B, p. 68)

Unlike the *Cornet,* the *Visions infernales* does not leave the reader entirely free to divine the unconscious impulses linking the poem's incompatible or deformed lexical elements. For the lyrical I, or narrator, assumes an active role here in interpreting his visions. He indicates his affective reaction ("l'image horrible") and adds emphasis through repetition and isolation of the symbolic signifier: *le démon*! The effect of the text is twofold. On the one hand, it evokes the latent fears of the dreamer, the empty trains and countryside suggesting the lyrical theme of death. But, at the same time, by superimposing a Christian interpretation upon the disordered associations surging from the unconscious, it endows an anachronistic, irrational world view with the psychic reality of dreams.

At this point, it might be relevant to digress on Jacob's use of symbolism. In "Voir sa mort dans sa vie" the lyrical I identifies an *employé des gares* and a *voyageur* as symbols of demoniality. But every station employee and every traveler in Jacob's poetry by no means signified *le démon,* or evil. And, in fact, the expressive force of the "symbols" in the poem cited above derived from the context, from the emergence of the lonely, threatening figures in a hallucinatory setting. For the most part, Jacob's religious poetry expanded the connotations of verbal signs through associations within the text, rather than through recourse to fixed symbolism. Indeed, even signs borrowed from traditional Christian mythology tended to receive new meanings from their integration in his poems.

Nevertheless, a few symbols reappeared with a constant significance in his writings, related especially to the kabbalistic image of the cosmos of concentric circles. In the *Visions infernales,* hell was represented by the figure of a ring "formée de deux serpents qui saignaient et qui ne pouvaient se mordre" (B, p. 84) and other signs belonging to the paradigm of infernal circles: "La table ronde et moi seul parlent. Or les fonds concentriques des assiettes... se précisent... tu es ici sur le chemin de l'enfer. Bosses concentriques de la mare." (B, p. 69) Circular bodies of water had similar connotations: "Au fond du monde, il y a quelque chose qui remue et qui attire comme le fond des bagues et celui des étangs." (B, p. 79) Yet, paradoxically, the circle also symbolized for Jacob the heavenly sphere, whose luminous center figured in the *Zohar* as a pearl. "Classique cheval ailé" contains this symbol, as well as an elaboration of the kabbalistic view of man, the microcosm enclosing the divine cosmic center:

> Pégase broutait l'herbe rare sur la colline
> où brillaient les saphirs, perles des nuits divines
> Ah! tu ne comprends pas! le pivot de l'esprit
> c'est un tout petit point au creux de l'estomac
> ... ...
> Comprendre, oh Dieu! comprendre faites que je comprenne
> Tu es un coin du monde où des palais de nacre
> préparent au poète des aurores du sacre:
> Comprendre!   (B, p. 238)

The most comprehensive representation of the poet's cosmological vision appeared in "Colimaçon." Both referents of this sign

— the snail and the spiral staircase — function as verbal emblems of the universe of concentric spheres. Each stanza of the poem presents the symbol and an allegorical description of its metaphysical significance. In the first, it embodies the circular ascent to heaven: "Colimaçon, le ciel en est la pointe!" (B., p. 216) In the second stanza, which alludes to the kabbalistic microcosm/macrocosm, the cosmological spiral becomes the human intestinal passage, source of poetry for Max Jacob: [12]

> Colimaçon, le chemin de Jacob
> lent à gravir on tire à six chevaux
> pour extirper entre têtes et ventres
> les mots écrits sur les intestinaux.

The next four verses equate the figure with the inferno: "Colimaçon se prend à la renverse / la pointe en bas c'est l'enfer odorant." And, in its conclusion, the poem summarizes its mystical interpretation of the contemplated emblem: "Colimaçon n'es-tu forme des mondes / très pure en haut flamme et bitume en bas." Such overt symbolical reference to extra-textual concepts reduces ambiguity, so that the contrast between the poles of enigma and confession (in the form of explanation) diminishes proportionally. In "Colimaçon" the cognitive function predominates; in "Voir sa mort dans sa vie" the resistance of opaque signs to the speaker's arbitrary rationalization increased affective and poetic expressivity.

Let us now consider a reverse function of the stylistic contrast of confessional and enigmatic devices, the focus on thematic antithesis rather than complementarity. As in the *Défense*'s "La Messe du visionnaire," in a number of Jacob's later poems the poetic speaker's statements in the confessional mode oppose the deciphering of hidden significations. Among his *Derniers poèmes*, for example, there is a group of visionary prose poems under the heading "Microcosme et macrocosme." Through typically Surrealist techniques — the juxtaposition of unlike lexical elements, the evocation of semantic metamorphoses, the predominance of disjunctive and elliptical syntax — these short texts suggest latent meanings, but do not explicitly provide them. The first piece consists of one line, which grammatically equates two disparate signifiers: "La puce est un homard

---

[12] See above, p. 53.

minuscule." (DP, p. 140) The reader's response may be amusement at the surprising identification, sensual pleasure on the imaginary visual level, or wonder at a possible mystical correspondence of such logically distinct signs. But the last poem of the series offers the emotive reaction of the lyrical I to his own exercises in linguistic orphism:

> J'ai passé mon lourd sommeil à essayer de déchiffrer des pages d'imprimerie. Un rêve! le livre était trop loin de moi et les mots trop fins, trop petits: Anaximène, salsifis, tireligne, péjoratif. Un rêve? oui et plus un cauchemar!

The affective value of this final exclamation, expressing not only the futility but the anguish of visionary practices, is augmented by its opposition to the preceding mystical context. And, similarly, in "Balistique et kabalistique" the speaker's renunciation of occultism for orthodox faith:

> Kabbale! à tes jeux de kabyles
> non! je ne veux pas être habile.
> Mes yeux aux yeux de Jésus-Christ!
> Tous mes cris et tous mes écrits
> au carrefour du crucifix!   (HC, p. 60)

would be less compelling, if it did not follow upon a concrete manifestation of orphic imagery:

> Sa couronne est de vingt-deux lettres!
> Le monde est un livre pour Lui
> Dix grillages cachent Sa tête
> Sa baignoire est dix infinis.

The tendency toward enigma in Jacob's religious poetry did not always translate his belief in the mystical signification of language. In predominantly confessional poems, oneiric sequences frequently served as objective correlatives, reinforcing lyrical themes. The poetic speaker of "Corpus Christi," in supplicating God, directly expresses the Christian motif of bodily corruption:

> or c'est Ton Corps et non le mien que je désire
> œil du démon cils de génisse
> tu ne m'annonces que le vice   (B, p. 136)

Further on in the poem, the same motif is conveyed by a hallucinatory tableau:

> Dragon je ne vous lègue pas l'asphalte de ma peau
> pour que vous y dansiez sur des échafauds
> le tango ou la valse des voieries.

These lines are particularly effective in evoking the sentiment of guilt, because, as in the poems of the *Cornet,* the absence of a logical transition and the discontinuity of the images contribute to the suggestion of discomfiture. With a homologous structure, a poem entitled "Examen de conscience" projects the speaker's sense of unworthiness, confessed directly to Christ: "Que crier? quoi? vers Vous / qui connaissez mes hontes?" (B, p. 147) through a sequence of dream-like metamorphoses of the lyrical I: [13]

> Et moi cet homme sur cette chaise
> un ver coupé en deux qui biaise
> une ville saccagée après reddition
> et qu'on vend à l'encan avec la couverture
> la graisse les faux regards et les promesses.

The unity here does not derive from the extension of a metaphor whose elements symbolize particular qualities of the lyrical I, but from the relation of disintegration that connects the transformations, whose cumulative effect corresponds to the speaker's *hontes.* Thus, Surrealistic images increased the emotive and poetic force of Jacob's devotional poems, suggesting intensity of experience that could not be expressed through purely abstract concepts.

Like the opposition of enigma and confession, Jacob's contrasts of burlesque and confessional techniques had both complementary and antithetical semantic functions. Humorous word-play, for instance, could formally actualize a lyrical motif, such as the absurdity of material existence: "Elle me fut trop tracassière, terre théière en terre de fer." (DP, p. 85) In "L'Homme est seul" the extended development of this characteristically burlesque device determines the poem's structure and significance. The opening lines introduce the central theme through the polarity of two nearly

---

[13] For a discussion of transformation as a theme and stylistic device in Jacob's early poetry, see Oxenhandler, pp. 224-27.

homophonous words, "pas assez" and "panacée," to suggest a double view of solitude: "La solitude et pas assez! il nous faudrait la gangue, / la solitude, ô panacée! et ce manque m'efflanque." (DP, p. 81) In the course of the text, the lyrical I reflects upon the ironies of solitude, which offers a spiritual panacea: "Ah! seulement que je m'absorbe / dans ma guérite ou porche," if it entails purification of the soul along with the social isolation: "Dieu me garde en ma Bastille / m'y tortille comme Robinson dans son île" that does not guarantee against sinful temptation: "tant est soluble ma pauvre âme." Counterpointing these emotive confessions, the discontinuous rhythm established in the first lines generates a series of internal rhymes, prolonging the effect of the initial pun. Each of these alliterations or assonances echoes the earlier thematic focus on duality, by evoking contradictory attributes of the poetic speaker: "au moindre Sélam d'un quidam / mon intégrité s'entame... crocodile, incivil et viril... graine et gangrène / avec deux noms matricule, ridicule: un état civil / Incongru, paru, disparu." The effect of these unexpected associations based on sound is comic, but in a disconcerting manner, since they also represent a schism in the lyrical I. A variant of the opening word-play concludes the poem:

> Un homme est seul, un cétacé!
> un homme est seul, pas assez!
> s'il l'était davantage
> de sa cellule avec lui, Son Dieu ferait partage.

If the homophonous sense of "cétacé" is considered, the opposition between the rhyme words "c'est assez" / "pas assez" recalls the antithesis of sufficient (spiritual) and insufficient (material) solitude. The double reading of "cétacé" further implies spirit versus matter, since it opposes man's choice of isolation to the retreat of an animal. The last couplet enlarges the paradox by means of a classical conceit: perfect solitude, after all, necessitates the company of God.

"L'Homme est seul" receives expressive power from the coupling of the conventionally incompatible qualities of humor and anguish. The poem's word-play reinforces, phonemically, the lyrical motif of contradiction. At the same time, this sense of incongruity is mirrored in the poem's stylistic structure. For while the lyrical I considers the serious moral and theological dilemma of spiritual perfectionment, his reflections are constantly disrupted by illogical associations of sounds, producing a startling effect not far from burlesque. As a consequence of these apparently uncontrolled verbal digressions, the poetic speaker becomes an ironic figure. But the contrast of his comic and confessional tones only serves to highlight the meaning of the text, since the poem is about a man tormented by duality. If the poet's religious faith were perfected, then undoubtedly its poetic translation would take a more harmonious form.

Discordancy permeates every level of Jacob's religious poetry. So that the contrast of burlesque and confessional techniques, supporting thematic opposition, often makes emotive professions of remorse or faith the object of parody within the text. This ironic intention is explicitly announced in the title "Confession de l'auteur — Son portrait en crabe." The reader cannot trust the affirmations of a poetic speaker who views his own spirituality as inferior to a crab's: "Vous avez, maître cancre, jambe et pieds ogivaux; / je me voudrais gothique et ne suis qu'en sabots." (DP, p. 51) In another instance, a revealing title and colloquialism insure a parodic counterpoint to the superficially devotional language of the "Vantardises d'un marin breton ivre":

> Attendez!... Dieu, c'est Jésus-Christ
> C'est moi!... c'est moi!... je vous le dis.
> ... ...
> Je suis Dieu! écoutez mon cri:
> Je vous invite au Paradis. (DP, p. 71)

A shift from first person confession to second person exhortation may dramatize opposing motifs, as in "Taie divine," where the speaker's sense of mystical union with God:

> voilà le miracle où j'en suis
> depuis Vous-moi et depuis
> moi-Vous, ma grande ambition céleste

is undermined by an unexpected accusation of impiety: "Ce que tu fais, ce que tu dis / te fait masquer le Paradis." (DP, p. 75)[14] "Eternité dans l'enfer" parodically alternates a suffering penitent's eloquent diction:

---

[14] For further discussion of this poem, see below, p. 102.

> ... Sans que ma peau fumant sous les aigres tisons
> ait le soulagement même des pâmoisons
> brûlé vif et pour mieux souffrir ressuscitant

with the colloquial syntax and vocabulary of an abrupt interruption:

> tu peux te retourner sur ton lit maintenant
> Après tant de mensonges et tant de jeux de l'oie
> tu la trouves enfin la posture qui est "toi!" (HC, p. 93)

to contrast the motifs of devotion and *tartuferie*.

Parody of religious themes, through the contrast of burlesque and confessional effects, typifies the self-consciousness of Jacob's poetry.[15] If the *Cornet à dés* parodied the style of other writers, the later poems constantly referred to his own *écriture* with a parodic intention. His "Réponse à l'apparition," for example, satirizes the poetic method of his devotional poetry. A footnote to the title alludes specifically to three of Jacob's works: "1. Voir *La Défense de Tartuffe, Saint Matorel* et *Le Cornet à dés* du même auteur." (B, p. 220)[16] In the opening lines of the "Réponse" an impersonal description of a village reminiscent of the poet's native Quimper suggests, perhaps, the visual element of his style, evaluated as passable: "La description est assez belle." Then the text shifts to the second person, admonishing the writer of the footnoted volumes:

> mais, je vous en prie, par piété
> effacez à la sandaraque
> Dieu passant derrière les baraques.
> Etant partout, Dieu n'est pas là
> et fût-il un jour quelque part
> il choisirait un autre endroit
> que ménageries et bazars
> de profils, de faces, de dos
> et votre nom sur calicot.

---

[15] Parody creates the ironic distance between writer and text, propounded by Jacob in his *Art poétique*, p. 74: "Dans les grandes œuvres, il y a autant d'ironie que de candeur, même les plus tragiques. L'ironie qui se laisse ou ne se laisse pas voir donne à l'œuvre cet éloignement sans lequel il n'y a pas 'création'."

[16] This spelling of "Tartuffe" corresponds to the orthograph of the original manuscript of the *Défense*, cf. above, p. 72, n. 7.

Several qualities of Jacob's devotional poems are inferred here. God appearing behind the stalls of a circus or fair alludes to their mixture of the mystical and the everyday. The tendency toward histrionic changes of tone and self-advertisement are indicated in the last two lines cited. Yet, Jacob's irony extends even beyond the obvious satire, for within the argument of his imaginary critic, there is a logical impossibility: "Etant partout, Dieu n'est pas là." Evidently, if God is everywhere, he may be perceived among "ménageries et bazars." And so the parody includes the poet's own defense!

This self-referential aspect consisted not only of allusions to the poet, to his works, to the reader, but also of depictions of the act of writing. Thus, "Classique cheval ailé" draws attention to the progress of its own creation: "Tu écris? et tu ne sais pas ce qu'est un homme / Je pleure! et toi tu ris!" (B, p. 238) If these unidentified first and second persons are assumed to represent the poet criticizing himself, then the text points to a crucial preoccupation of modern poetics: the realization that the lyrical I (linguistic subject) cannot correspond exactly to the subjectivity of the writer. But for Jacob, although he was acutely aware of that dichotomy, another issue predominated. He was preoccupied with the ethical and theological implications of the split between the poetic speaker and the poet. Parodic references to his *écriture* often questioned the morality of poems exposing his sins. In "Trop petit trop grand" he summed up the conflict in an ingenious *calembour*: "Emoi des maux / j'ai peur des mots." (HC, p. 103) Self-referential elements also stressed the futility of art — even devotional art — as an instrument of salvation. A poem entitled "Jugement dernier" thus interrupts the verses of a sermon-like discourse on the apocalypse with a paragraph of prose, in which the poet castigates himself for writing:

> Mais laissons tous ces vers, ils importent peu à mon salut; c'est à vous, mon Dieu, que je m'adresse avec mon salut. L'épouvante devrait emplir mon cœur au lieu que par cet art je m'enivre et me vante. A qui donc plus qu'à moi le Jugement fait peur! Quoi, le ciel et le monde me verront dans mes hontes et c'est sur des vers que je compte? Ma vie s'étalera devant le monde entier, devant Dieu et devant les anges avant d'être précipité où le veut la justice et mon

> intempérance. Monsieur pensait en vers! C'est une belle excuse. (DP, p. 89)

Then the lyrical confession in verse resumes, as if there had been no disruption! As a result of these parodic contrasts of confession and burlesque, of the penitent and the impostor, of devotional poetry and the parody of devotional poetry, the reader is left in a state of doubt. Not as to the religious orientation of the texts, but regarding the resolution of their dramatic tension.

We have seen how the evolution of Jacob's poetry followed a course quite different from the fictional stages of the Matorel/Tartufe myth. By retaining his early tendencies toward the burlesque and the enigmatic, Jacob succeeded in avoiding the "Lamartinian" sentimentality, which he feared at the outset of his conversion. The spiritual experience he transposed into poetry was one of conflict, of movement, of process, reflected aesthetically in a structure of stylistic contrasts: The opposition of enigmatic imagery and confessional interpretation, as well as the emotive refutation of oneirism and word-play, corresponded to the occult and orthodox poles of his metaphysics. Juxtaposition of confession and burlesque reflected the struggles of conversion, the self-doubts of the penitent, the contradictions of the devotional poet. While the persistence of irony in Jacob's religious poetry has been taken as a sign of insincerity,[17] if his poetic method is to be interpreted as an indication of his faith, it might just as reasonably be considered a figure of his aversion to complacency and facile acceptance of dogma. In fact, it would have been inauthentic for his poems not to embody a dialectic. So the criticism of Hubert Fabureau perceptively recognized the antithetical tendencies of Jacob's style, but unfortunately misjudged their value: "L'ironie détruit en lui l'enthousiasme. Avec une joie funèbre, il met au supplice son âme de

---

[17] André Salmon, in *Max Jacob, Poète, Peintre, Mystique et Homme de Qualité* (Paris: René Girard, 1927), pp. 11-12, defended Jacob against the accusations of contemporaries who considered his humor contradictory to faith: "C'est parce qu'ils n'entendent pas bien cette Poésie qu'ils se persuadent d'aimer, qu'on les peut voir ainsi mettre en doute la qualité de ta conversion.... Je vois très bien Max Jacob faisant à Dieu une imitation de Monseigneur. Pourquoi pas? Tout le mal du monde vient peut-être de ce que la fausse sagesse et la sotte gravité des hommes très bien, tout ce qu'il y a de bien, ont empeché Dieu d'oser rire."

poète que torturent alors la parodie et les caprices burlesques, la mystification et les jeux cubistes." [18] Regretting the loss of "un poète élégiaque, animé de sentiments sincères," Fabureau failed to appreciate the poetic force achieved through discordance.

Max Jacob's religious poetry was indeed the expression of a Tartufe, but of a Tartufe whom the poet reinvented according to his Pascalian vision: "De même qu'un homme qui se veùt de la gravité se donne la mine de l'avoir pour acquérir le reste, celui qui prétend à la perfection religieuse en aura d'abord les apparences.... Tartuffe est apprenti, on le croit comédien." [19] (DT, p. 295) The voice we hear in his texts is that of the apprentice, not the actor. The clown, after all, was at the altar.

---

[18] *Max Jacob: son œuvre* (Paris: Editions de la Nouvelle revue critique, 1935), pp. 76-77.

[19] This statement appears in a manuscript entitled "Défense de Tartuffe ou Portrait de l'auteur en martyr" dated 1917, but published for the first time in Blanchet's appendix to the 1964 edition of the *Défense*.

M. de Max offrait tous ses profils à chacun des deux partis comme autant de prismes géants.

                MAX JACOB, *Le Cornet à dés*

One constantly notices in very active natures a tendency to pose, or if the pose has become a second self a preoccupation with the effect they are producing.

                W. B. YEATS, *Autobiography*

Chapter IV

DIALOGISM

Readers of Max Jacob, invariably, notice the conversational facility of his style. In describing his talent as a novelist, André Billy praised the mimetic genius "d'un contemplateur dans la mémoire de qui les gestes et les paroles s'inscrivaient comme dans un appareil enregistreur";[1] referring to both his prose and verse, Billy admired Jacob's gift of "une 'diction' simple, naturelle, rapide, d'une vivacité entraînante, tout à l'opposé du style littéraire et artiste. *Cela n'a pas l'air écrit, mais plutôt parlé.*"[2] Summing up the stylistic processes of *La Côte,* Jacob's first volume of poetry, Jean de Palacio remarked: "C'est un style se rapprochant le plus possible de celui de la conversation, le *sermo pedestris* des Anciens."[3] It was Jean Rousselot, p. 176, however, who recognized the significance of this definitive trait of Jacob's writing. In a discussion of the proliferous correspondence of the poet, he wrote: "Aussi bien, ces milliers de lettres font-elles partie intégrante d'une œuvre qui, poème ou roman, drame ou pastiche, confession ou essai, se veut avant tout *dialogue,* en appelle constamment par son écriture même (l'apostrophe, l'interjection, la parenthèse, les points de suspension) et sa tonalité (la blague, la confidence, la familiarité) au jugement, à la critique, à l'adhésion d'autrui; exige à tout le moins une réponse et s'identifie, dans tous les domaines qu'elle aborde, à une entreprise de prosélytisme autant qu'à une création de l'esprit."

---

[1] *Max Jacob,* rev. ed., Poètes d'aujourd'hui, No. 3 (Paris: Pierre Seghers, 1945), p. 40.
[2] *Idem.* Italics are my emphasis.
[3] "Un Précurseur inattendu de Max Jacob," p. 193.

Thus, the conversational quality of Max Jacob's style exposes an underlying intention of dialogue.

Instances of spoken language are as numerous in Jacob's religious poetry as in other forms of his writing. Apostrophes, both literary and colloquial, occur regularly:

> Douce mère de Dieu!... serais-je encor vivant? (DP, p. 45)
> O parchemin! O parchemin!
> C'est toi qui montres le chemin. (HC, p. 87)

Parentheses and points of suspension suggest confidential asides to imaginary listeners:

> (après tout, peut-être n'est-ce que du théâtre?) (DP, p. 52)
> Quand je revins... c'est moi qui parle et pourquoi pas?...
> (HC, p. 44)

Interjections, as well as adverbs indicating a time or place contemporaneous with the actual moment of speech, underscore the presence of a speaking subject:

> Ici, je m'arrête car je ne peux pas
> m'élever à l'âme. Ah! je ne peux pas... (DP, p. 66)
> Hors! çà! enfuyez-vous, noirceurs (DP, p. 74)

As a rule, several signs of spoken language converge to reinforce the conversational effect. For example, interjection, ellipsis, and indirect interrogation:

> Alors!... la mort est déjà là? (DP, p. 85)

And in the following lines, the combination of ellipsis, disjunctive syntax, repeated demonstratives, and a familiar vocabulary:

> Coupable ou non? c'en est triste à vomir. (DP, p. 83)
> c'est contre qui en somme ou plutôt c'est pourquoi
> ce bouclier que j'ai gris et noir comme un toit? (DP, p. 52)

Considered in their totality, the prevalent marks of spoken language constitute a rhetorical device unifying Jacob's religious poetry. To refer to this figure, we shall employ the term "dialogism," which Fontanier defined as the representation of direct speech: "Le *Dia-*

logisme consiste à rapporter directement et tels qu'ils sont censés sortir de la bouche, des discours que l'on prête à ses personnages, ou que l'on se prête à soi-même dans telle ou telle circonstance." [4] Jacob's dialogism was a sign of his modernism, since in the twentieth century the inclusion of attributes of spoken language in poetry has passed from an innovation to a convention. Critics have been particularly interested in distinguishing the modes of dialogism employed outside the drama, in delineating, for instance, the specificity of the dramatic monologue, the soliloquy, the psychological monologue, and so forth.[5] Nevertheless, the broad definition of Fontanier remains most useful to our study of Jacob. For his poems mix these different orientations of dialogism, in complete and fragmentary dialogues and monologues. Yet every variant of the figure shares common features: the marks of spoken language indicate, explicitly or implicitly, the presence of two interlocutors, a first and second person.

The constant features of dialogism have an aesthetic consequence; that is, they contribute to the dramatic quality of Jacob's religious poetry. The opposition of two grammatical persons (regardless of their notional identity) produces psychological tension. Although few of Jacob's texts conform to the precise limits of dramatic monologue, a number of the observations made in Robert Langbaum's study of that genre apply to his poems. Modern poetry, according to Langbaum, has assimilated the major attributes of Victorian dramatic monologue, which itself adopted the romantic tendency to subordinate "analytic reflection," while emphasizing experience or "imaginative apprehension."[6] The poetic speaker has come to resemble a "character" whose address has a "dialogue-like style." (pp. 52-57) This effect clearly characterizes Jacob's poems.

---

[4] Pierre Fontanier, *Les Figures du discours,* Collection Science de l'homme (Paris: Flammarion, 1968), p. 375.

[5] It is interesting that Edouard Dujardin, *Le Monologue intérieur, son apparition, ses origines, sa place dans l'œuvre de James Joyce* (Paris: Albert Messein, 1931), p. 79, who defined interior monologue as the reproduction of prelogical thought, as in Surrealist automatic writing, named Jacob as an early elaborator of the technique.

[6] Robert Langbaum, *The Poetry of Experience, The Dramatic Monologue in Modern Literary Tradition* (London: Chatto and Windus, 1957), p. 35. In the rest of this paragraph, page references to this edition are included in the text.

In the dramatic monologue, moreover, the aspect of characterization causes a split in the speaker's and the poet's consciousness; the reader, therefore, vacillates between sympathy with and judgment of the "character." (p. 96) Especially pertinent to Jacob's religious lyrics is Langbaum's suggestion that the control of sympathy or "suspension of disbelief" functions effectively in the dramatization of religious convictions the reader may not share. (pp. 104-106) By incorporating dramatic movement through dialogism, Jacob's poetry, like dramatic monologue, represents an existential experience, whose outcome is not known before the end of the poem. A good example is "L'Adoration nocturne au Sacré-Cœur de Montmartre," where the speaker is concretely situated in front of the cathedral: "C'est ici ta maison et ta capitale; / Comment les vitraux n'éclatent-ils pas?" and his advance toward the altar, accompanied by a monologue, determines the progression of the poem: "Ne parlons pas, marchons tout bas." (DT, pp. 183-84) In this way, Jacob presents not his reflections upon a spiritual dilemma, but the tension of the conflict itself.

Interestingly enough, the dramatic attitude of Jacob's dialogism has roots in an ancient as well as a modern aesthetic. Since the Psalms and the Book of Job, religious lyrics have recorded prayers spoken aloud to a divine listener. In the sixteenth and seventeenth centuries, the representation of spoken language was a device used consciously in the devotional poetry of England and France to produce the dramatic identification considered essential to mystical contemplation. Studying the English and French traditions, respectively, Louis L. Martz and Terence C. Cave have shown that the structure of devotional poems paralleled the method of religious meditation outlined in devotional treatises of the period. Both authors point out the function of the colloquial style and of rhetorical features typical of direct speech (interrogation, invocation, imperativeness) as a means of dramatizing theological points.[7] There can be no doubt of Max Jacob's familiarity with the tradition of spiritual exercises, since he faithfully employed Saint François de Sales's *Introduction à la vie dévote* as a guide to religious medita-

---

[7] Louis L. Martz, *The Poetry of Meditation, A Study in English Religious Literature of the Seventeenth Century* (New Haven: Yale Univ. Press, 1954), pp. 29-30, 37-38, 323-24; Cave, *Devotional Poetry*, pp. 33-34.

tion. And in this manual, Saint François insisted upon the efficacy of dialogue in devotional practices: "Il est bon d'user de colloque, et parler tantôt à Notre-Seigneur, tantôt aux Anges et aux personnes représentées aux mystères, aux Saints et à soi-même, à son cœur, aux pécheurs et même aux créatures insensibles, comme l'on voit que David fait en ses Psaumes, et les autres Saints, en leurs méditations et oraisons." [8]

The implications, then, of Jacob's dialogism reach out in multiple directions. But my analysis in this chapter deals with the meanings suggested by the figure within the poetic texts. Rousselot explained the marks of dialogue in Jacob's writing as an appeal "au jugement, à la critique, à l'adhésion d'autrui" motivated by the desire to proselytize. Applied to his letters, in which Max Jacob openly tried to convert his friends to Catholicism, this judgment is correct. But in the poems, the problem becomes more complex. Unlike the correspondent, the poet does not always address his reader directly. That is, the interlocutors — both first and second persons — of the monologues and dialogues of Jacob's poetry have fictional identities. Furthermore, although the linguistic function of second person statements is generally conative (indicating the motivation of persuasion), the degree of conation may be modified in a given context by the focus on other verbal functions, such as emotive and poetic orientations. [9] So that the instances of dialogism in Jacob's poetry constitute a discourse within the total discourse of the poem addressed by the poet to the reader.

In interpreting the significance of the rhetorical figure, I have been influenced by Emile Benveniste's discussion of the function of dialogue. In *Problèmes de linguistique générale,* Benveniste calls attention to the obvious yet overlooked fact that the concept of subjectivity, whether in phenomenology or psychology, relates to the exercise of language: "C'est dans l'instance de discours où *je* désigne

---

[8] Collection Livre de vie (Paris: Editions du Seuil, 1962), p. 79.
[9] I use these terms in the sense of Roman Jakobson, "Linguistics and Poetics," in *Style in Language,* ed. Thomas A. Sebeok (Cambridge, Mass.: M.I.T. Press, 1960), pp. 353-57. The "poetic" orientation, or focus on language itself, has yet to be adequately clarified in respect to the "stylistic" function; for a discussion of the problem, see Michael Riffaterre, *Essais de stylistique structurale* (Paris: Flammarion, 1971), pp. 154-56.

le locuteur que celui-ci s'énonce comme 'sujet'." [10] But the "je" is not solipsistic. The identity of the subject depends on the polarization of dialogue: "La conscience de soi n'est possible que si elle s'éprouve par contraste. Je n'emploie *je* qu'en m'adressant à quelqu'un, qui sera dans mon allocution un *tu*. C'est cette condition de dialogue qui est constitutive de la *personne,* car elle implique en réciprocité que je deviens *tu* dans l'allocution de celui qui à son tour se désigne par *je*." (p. 260) Max Jacob's religious poetry exhibits an intense awareness of the dialectic of speaking persons, defined by Benveniste as the linguistic embodiment of identity: "C'est dans une réalité dialectique englobant les deux termes ["moi"/"l'autre"] et les définissant par relation mutuelle qu'on découvre le fondement linguistique de la subjectivité." (p. 260) Dialogism in Jacob's writing goes beyond either proselytism or the mimetic purpose of reproducing spoken language. Through his exploration of the relation of first and second persons in discourse, Jacob reveals the interdependence of subjectivity and otherness.

At the outset of our reading of the poet's monologues and dialogues, an obvious question presents itself. Who are the interlocutors? Since we are considering religious poetry, a logical expectation would be an exchange between a speaker and God. In fact, such a dialogue occurs in a number of poems which follow the conventions of devotional poetry. As Martz, p. 38, demonstrated, the thematic structure of this mode resembles traditional methods of meditation: the "composition" of a subject or place precedes its "analysis" and the final affective "colloquy," demonstrating the will of the meditator to achieve union with God. For the theme of his meditative poems, as a rule, Jacob chose subjects prescribed by Saint François in the *Introduction*. (See above, p. 40) A poem entitled "Jugement dernier" illustrates the characteristic elements of the devotional dialogue addressed to God. It begins with a visual evocation of the Last Judgment and of Christ transformed from father to avenging judge. Jacob's text profits from the freedom to express emotion at any moment in the meditation — encouraged by Saint François, p. 78: "Il ne faut jamais retenir les affections" —

---

[10] Bibliothèque des Sciences Humaines (Paris: Gallimard, 1966), p. 262. In the rest of this paragraph, page references to this edition are included in the text.

and interrupts the composition of the tableau with the exclamation: "A qui donc plus qu'à moi le Jugement fait peur!" (DP, p. 89) In the analysis, the idea of the Last Judgment is concretized through a comparison with the actuality of occupied France ("cette année quarante") and the ravages of war. The concluding lines, evoking resolutions and emotions provoked by contemplation, typify the closing colloquies of the devotional tradition:

> O mon Dieu, faites que je vive pour ce jour.
> A votre aide, ô mon Dieu voyez que je recours.
> Et faites en tous temps à toutes les minutes
> Qu'à l'oubli par Satan je ne sois plus en butte
> Que tout me quitte, ô Dieu, mais mon pas le souci
> Du jour où de vous, Dieu, je recevrai l'acquit!

The function of the preceding second person statements is primarily conative and the relation supplicatory, for the first person is subordinate to the second.[11]

The rapport between the "je" and the divine interlocutor, however, is not stable. In an "Examen de conscience," also evoking final judgment, the first person, overcome by remorse, does not close his meditation with the conventional prayer; instead he invokes his incertitude and incapacity to establish the dialogue with God: "Que crier? quoi? vers Vous / qui connaissez mes hontes?" (B, p. 147) A similar sense of separation pervades the following invocation, in which the contrast of a mystical and colloquial vocabulary suggests the difficulty of the spiritual quest in the material setting:

> Mon Dieu, je poursuis ton regard
> comme on poursuivrait une affaire:
> où es-tu? et sous quel hangar?   (HC, p. 60)

The attitude of the speaker toward the divine interlocutor appears still more equivocal in "Chrétiens et païens," where burlesque and confessional tones interpenetrate, as the "je" offers trivial excuses to an angry, paternalistic divinity:

> "Les païens ont pour moi plus de respect que vous!"
> M'avez-vous dit, Seigneur, au réveil de ma sieste.

---

[11] Cf. Jakobson, "Linguistics and Poetics," p. 303.

> C'est vrai que, ce matin-là, j'avais communié.
> Mais après, que de courses! avenue de Villier...
>
> (DT, p. 171)

The tension in the dialogue intensifies, when God becomes the speaking subject, transforming the lyrical I into a second person, an other: "On ne saurait servir deux maîtres à la fois, / m'a répondu le Dieu dont je connais la voix." (HC, p. 44) In this instance of discourse, the "je" who appeared in the preceding lines of the poem as a penitent, is suddenly objectified in the divine interlocutor's exhortation as a hypocrite.

There is a movement in Jacob's dialogism to obliterate the distinction between the self and the divine Other, that is the poetic transposition of mystical aspiration. In "Taie divine," the "je" is metamorphosed into a reflection of the divine presence, embodied in the kabbalistic image of a pearly white spot, equally symbolic of the Eucharist: [12]

> La tache est descendue en blanc
> nacrée comme un intérieur d'huître
> je ne me vois que sous sa vitre   (DP, p. 75)

The title suggests the interpretation of the mirror imagery ("intérieur d'huître," "vitre") as a metaphor for God's vision, shared for the moment by the speaker. The theme of mystical union, its desirability and impossibility, is given a linguistic form in the poem in the arbitrary attachment of the two interlocutors, the lyrical I and God. The hyphen, by its very nature (underscored in the French expression "trait d'union"), simultaneously implies unity and separation:

> voilà le miracle où j'en suis
> depuis Vous-moi et depuis
> moi-Vous, ma grande ambition célestique

The coupling of the pronouns signifies the awareness that the "je" can become the transparent reflection of the divine Other only if

---

[12] "L'Adoration nocturne au Sacré-Cœur de Montmartre" offers a concordance for the white spot as the Host: "L'hostie est une tache qui s'étend sur l'univers" (DT, p. 184); as does the meditation "Crainte et respect": "Dieu est cette immense tache blanche qui est partout." (DT, p. 219)

subjectivity is transcended. That is, as the text indicates, in the death of the body: "depuis moi mort que l'on exhume," which allows reunion of the soul with God. The poem's concluding exhortation, however, reestablishes the dialogue or distinction of the "je" and the "tu" and the state of duality (man/God) inseparable from the living condition: "Ce que tu fais, ce que tu dis / te fait masquer le Paradis."

In association with poetic equivalences, the "je"/"tu" dialectic frequently concretizes the motif of impossible mystical union. The closing lines of the significantly entitled poem "Impuissance," for example, creates an ambiguity in which the "je" and the divine interlocutor approach identity:

> la lanterne le soir le soir après l'émeute
> Diogène cherche un homme c'est Lui
> c'est moi c'est Vous c'est Vous
> Seigneur très Pur que je cherche comme la santé.
> 				(B, p. 145)

Diogenes looks for a man, and this man is He. (The capitalization, of course, suggests divinity.) In the next line, three pronominal phrases ("c'est moi c'est Vous c'est Vous") echo, on the metrical, grammatical, morphological, and syntactical levels, the binary measure "c'est Lui." This linguistic correspondence infers a metaphorical identification of the pronouns: He, I, You. For a moment, then, semantic ambivalence permits a double interpretation of the figure of Diogenes as the speaker seeking either God or himself. The divine Other and the "je" seem to merge. But only tentatively, for in the last verse, the distinction between the first person and the divine interlocutor is reinstated, since the vocative "Seigneur" makes God the specific object of the speaker's quest.

The paradox accounting for the identity/non-identity of the lyrical I and the divine interlocutor is the Christian doctrine of an immanent and transcendent God. One of Jacob's most explicit developments of this theme is found in "Les Deux Christ." Like "Taie divine," the poem plays with images of reflection to convey the idea of the speaker finding himself in God and God in himself:

> Te cachant, Jésus, tu me caches!
> Si je veux connaître mon cœur

> c'est ton image ô Photographe
> que j'obtiens au Révélateur. (HC, p. 63)

Here again, syntactical, morphological, and grammatical equivalence of the personal pronouns "te" and "me," "mon" and "ton," suggest the identity, or at least the desire for union, of the lyrical I and the divine Other. But dialogue also maintains the separation of the interlocutors, situating God outside the "je": "Si je t'entends et te regarde / c'est bien que Tu vis hors de nous." In the final lines, the unfulfilled wish for the reunion of the divinity within and without is reiterated: "Que les deux Jésus se rejoignent / l'âme a surpris son patrimoine."

But the divine Other is not the only interlocutor whom the "je" addresses. Inversely parallel to the dialogue with God is the dialogue with Satan. And while the speaker generally supplicates the former, he exhorts the latter:

> Voilà combien d'années, de milliers de semaines
> Que je connais vos noms,
> Cavaliers du démon,
> Vos commandants, vos capitaines!
> Mais le Tien, Rayonnant, redore
> A rajeuni, éclabousse le mal
> Jéhovah, o Ieho! o Jahveh, Adonaï. (B, p. 132)

Corresponding to the tension created by the opposition of the "je" and "tu," there is a recurrent antithesis dividing the second persons of Jacob's religious poetry. From this polarization of the personified symbols of good and evil, metaphorical contrasts are generated. Such as, light and dark in "Taie divine," the "tache blanche" opposed to the "noirceurs" embodying demonic impulses and addressed antagonistically: "Hors! ça! enfuyez-vous, noirceurs / qui souillez tout jusqu'à mon cœur." (DP, pp. 74-75) The dialogue with Satan menaces the opposing dialogue, for the lyrical I sometimes proves incapable of maintaining contact with the divine Other. Although the speaker of "Pas encore" invokes God at the outset of his penitent confession, his spiritual imperfection brings a response from the demonic interlocutor:

> Immortel génie, Dieu qui êtes partout,
> ... ...
> Je vous demande peu: donnez-moi quelque rente,

> Et qu'on me laisse seul avec mon grand ennui.
> Le diable répond: "C'est moi qui te tourmente!"
> (DT, p. 114)

For Jacob, duality implied the instability of the subject. When Satan usurps God's reply, he encroaches upon the identity of the divine interlocutor. But, at the same time, the subjectivity of the "je" appears threatened, for assuming control of the dialogue amounts to domination of the speaker's will. By responding to a penitent's prayer in "A Une Sainte le jour de sa fête," the demonic forces essentially take possession of the speaker's being, transforming the "je" into a tormented "tu":

> Je suis le diable et sa clique
> et c'est moi qui te réplique
> Pèche à droite, pèche à gauche
>   Tourne-toi comme tu veux
> Va! c'est chez moi que tu loges
>   tu n'appartiens pas à Dieu. (B, p. 247)

Visual evocations of demonic metamorphoses in the *Visions infernales* convey a similar sense of uncertain identity:

> Le moine qui étudie sa partie de hautbois pour une fête n'est moine que de robe, il a la figure d'un démon. Un prêtre me retient, il a des pattes griffues. (B, p. 46)

Analogously, in a poem entitled "Agonie," a shared mask becomes the metaphorical vehicle for the idea of usurped identity: "Satan mettait mon masque / le sien en mufle de tarasque." (DP, p. 86) This image also suggests a dialectic or interchange of subjectivity and otherness. For the opposition of personal (first person) and impersonal (third person) pronouns maintains a separation of the lyrical I and the devil, while grammatical apposition emphasizes their equivalence. It is because Satan, like God, is both immanent and transcendent that he has the power to become the "je." Thus, at the core of many of the speaker's dialogues with these figures lies an impulse to eliminate the distinction between the first and second persons, desired or feared, according to whether the "tu" is heavenly or demonic:

> Oh! ne me regarde pas comme si j'allais mourir car tu es moi-même et je te connais. L'Enfant! l'enfant vient-il du ciel ou de l'enfer? Souris, je te connaîtrai par ton sourire. (B, p. 76)

So that, finally, the "je" assumes the division opposing the two interlocutors: "De plus en plus lorsque Dieu t'avoisine / de plus en plus le diable te résine." (DP, p. 84)

Other interlocutors in Jacob's religious poetry participate in antitheses parallel to the God/Satan opposition. Categories of vocatives include natural and fabricated objects, animals, abstract concepts, and mythological figures, while humans are rarely addressed. "Les Cloches" illustrates the antagonistic tension among inanimate second persons. Church bells, standing metonymically for the Deity, are addressed in terms of supplication: "Pardonnez! pardonnez l'homme amer qui pardonne." (B, p. 267) This supplicatory invocation contrasts with a hortatory address to bells serving mundane purposes: "Cloches des wagons sourds, des roues / vous ne m'inspirez rien du tout."[13] The shift of tone in these second person statements suggests a symbolic opposition of the heavenly and the terrestrial. In the last line of the poem, a third vocative introduces the antithesis of the divine and the infernal. The syntax, which begins with an elliptical pause and a conjunction of contradiction or hesitation: "... Mais je pense à vous, casseroles," gives the "casseroles" a connotation of menace, an echo of the dantesque infernal decor, not denoted by the sign in its ordinary sense.[14] By focussing on the attitude of the lyrical I toward the object addressed, both the second and third vocatives serve primarily affective rather than conative functions. Respectively, they attribute to the speaker, indifference to earthly concerns and apprehension of danger.

---

[13] The exhortation probably refers metalinguistically to Jacob's burlesque mode of writing, which could be considered an "earthly" concern compared with his new emphasis on devotional themes. In "Les Cloches," the "cloches des wagons sourds" are associated metonymically with a voyage from Paris to Nantes and with the village of Saumur, all elements of a poem of the same collection, "La Saltimbanque en wagon de 3ᵉ classe" (B, p. 222), in which nonsensical sound play predominates.

[14] Although the "casseroles" take on this meaning syntagmatically in the text of the poem, they do participate in Jacob's paradigm of circular figures signifying hell. Cf. "L'Enfer": "Au bout l'eau dans la casserole, / Enfer où le jour ne dure." (B, p. 195)

Behind the personification of inanimate objects through direct address, there is the implicit signification of a mystical attitude. The world of the speaker in the poems is an animated universe inhabited by divisive forces. And the mystical view also manifests itself in the movement of the lyrical I toward union with the elements of the cosmos, through imagery: "Surnaturel, je me cramponne à ton drapeau de soie / que le grand vent me coule dans tes plis qui ondoient" (B, p. 151), and through dialogue. For in addressing inanimate vocatives, the lyrical I may invest them with affective meaning reflecting personal emotions (as in "Les Cloches"), thus tending toward another form of identification with the "tu," in this case, the phenomenal world.

It is not only the opposition of subject and object, interior and exterior reality, that is maintained through dialogism. The consciousness of duality is introjected into the lyrical I. Throughout Jacob's poetry, self-division is made explicit in physical imagery:

Deux dragons se battaient pour la victoire de Max (LC, p. 101)
Ma peau est divisée en deux cantons (B, 137)
main du Seigneur, pied de Satan (HC, p. 115)

As in traditional Christian literature of devotion, these images suggest an intimate relationship between the corruption of the body and the soul, between sickness and sin: [15]

> Au Pilori le Christ est dans mes hanches:
> démons jaseurs visent à mon delta
> Son Aube Epine fait mal quand il penche
> De là provient la douleur de mon foie. (HC, p. 13)

But in representing a divided physiology, they combine the Old Testament themes of self-deprecation and penitence with the New Testament motifs of the Passion and redemption. By stressing the physical presence of Christ, Jacob's imagery infers the sinner's potential salvation:

> Pour être en nous, l'Esprit, il doit être dehors
> au-dessus de Jésus, vrai mort en son linceul
> le Dieu Jésus vivant, rouge et vert pour moi seul.

---

[15] Cf. Cave, pp. 96-123.

> Du Paradis mon crâne est la coupole.
> J'ai mon double et six sens
> les six sens que me fit votre chair auréole.   (HC, p. 69)

The preceding lines of "Autour du calvaire" present a complex image of duality; not only is the speaker the double of Christ, but the latter has two forms, the material and the spiritual, which the speaker, correspondingly, incarnates.

These recurrent evocations of self-division complement the figure of dialogism in its dramatic emphasis on the dialectic of self-apprehension. By grammatically alternating first and second person pronouns, Jacob's texts reflect the projection of the self as an other and, reciprocally, the introjection of otherness into the self. In his religious poems, this rhetorical process is generally associated with the motif of moral judgment:

> C'est toi, passé non trépassé?
> C'est moi qui remonte à ta cible,
> moribond qui ne fus pas bon.
> ... ...
> Savoir quand tu étais sincère,
> vieux personnage de la terre:
> quand j'étais chaste et vertueux
> pour plaire à mon ange, à mon Dieu   (DP, p. 85)

Yet, in the preceding lines, the repeated shift of pronouns and tenses equally reveals the psychological problem of subjectivity in time. The introduction of the "tu" and of the verb in the imperfect implies the split of the past and present self, while the return of the "je" suggests the continuity of the subject.[16] In these monologues, the attitude of the "je" towards the "tu" is invariably remonstrative, and the second person statements, exhortatory. For example, if the lyrical I of an "Examen de conscience" seems at first hopeful about the chances for redemption: "Aveugle fou!

---

[16] This poem, whose title "Agonie" situates it in a context of Christian thought, nevertheless, evokes through its shift of persons an existential consciousness of self-division analogous to the "angoisse devant le passé" described by Jean-Paul Sartre, in *L'Etre et le néant* (Paris: Gallimard, 1943), pp. 70-71: "Et l'angoisse *c'est moi*, puisque par le seul fait de me porter à l'existence comme conscience d'être, je me fais *n'être pas* ce passé de bonnes résolutions *que je suis.*"

Pourtant Dieu me fit grâce" (DP, p. 84), viewing himself "objectively" as a second person, he finds himself condemned:

> suppose bien qu'à soixante ans passés
> tu vas mourir! Ah! que Jésus t'assiste!
> Il n'est pas beau ton linge damassé.

Underlying the moral antitheses (good and bad, saved and damned, pure and soiled) represented through the "je"/"tu" relationship is the dilemma of identity itself. In Jacob's poetry, the dialogues with the self indicate the instability of the subject. When the speaker projects himself as an other, in order to decide his theological fate, or *who he is,* he exposes himself as a "vieux personnage" playing a part: "Dieu sait tes tours et tes détours. / Dieu connaît mon hypocrisie." (DP, p. 85) In a poem entitled "Enfer," not only the past and present, but the future takes the form of a role to be assumed: "Ce qui demeure est le futur / Non le présent qui me désole." (B, p. 195) And yet, the "je" fears he may be transfixed in the part of the moment, attributed to himself as "tu":

> Qui peut prétendre à l'auréole?
> Pas toi! te vois-tu en étole,
> Disant la messe dans l'azur?
> Quoi! après tant de gaudrioles.

If the lyrical I regrets his inconsistency, nevertheless, he realizes that assuming a role is also the essential condition of reformation. Still, the dialogues with the self are deceiving precisely because the "tu," being a projection (or reflection) of the "je," cannot provide the sense of permanent being: "Vous avez cru voir un ange / Et c'était votre miroir." (LC, p. 47)

The irrepressible desire for an unchanging identity is communicated, at times, by the elimination of dialogism. We saw an equivalent movement of auto-destruction in the tendency of the "je" to become the second person interlocutor, when the "tu" referred to God or Satan. On occasion — as in the poem "Le Double... et plus!" — the "je" assumes not a self-reflective posture, but a veritable impersonal identity: "Ce n'est pas moi qui parle / c'est un grand cheval blanc." (HC, p. 49) To escape the interdependence of subjectivity and otherness, the dialectic of the "je" and the "tu," the lyrical I becomes an "il": "Et moi cet homme sur cette chaise." (B, p. 146) [17] But in Jacob's poems, identification with a third person does not offer a satisfactory alternative to instability. For the "il" is as protean as the "je" / "tu." A number of texts follow a similar pattern, in which a series of statements beginning with the phrase "Je suis" conclude with a predicate noun. However, like a parody of self-affirmation, the enumeration of disparate complements produces an effect of metamorphosis, culminating in non-identity:

> Je suis le vieux rempart qui chante à marée haute
> l'éternel rescapé, la toupie du Très-Haut.
> Je suis le double six et le double zéro   (HC, p. 46)
> Je suis la pie un couteau sur la manche
> Je suis l'auto qu'on sortait le dimanche
> Je suis perdu et j'écris au hasard
> Je suis caméléon et je suis un lézard   (DP, p. 13)

And reinforcing the motif of self-disintegration ("le double zéro," "caméléon") are the predominant deprecatory connotations of these transformations: "le fond d'artichaut cru, l'endive et le chaud-froid." (HC, p. 46)

If recurrent dialogism and metamorphoses (fictions, phantasms) prevent the stable subjectivity of the lyrical I, there is, nonetheless, one constant symbol of permanent being in Jacob's religious poetry. The way out of the labyrinth of reflections, signifying self-consciousness, is the literal obliteration of the "je," or death. In preceding pieces, we have seen both the mirror and the mask convey the theme of transient identity. In the poem entitled "Face," their meaning is reversed; a mirror having lost its silvering and a death mask suggest the ultimate objectivization of the "je" into a "tu":

> Toi qui par les mondains fus si souvent raillé,
> miroir au tain perdu de froide indifférence,
> si de l'Esprit la mort ce sont les relevailles
> montre à tous, masque mort, ta juste ressemblance
>
>   (HC, p. 45)

---

[17] For the distinction between personal and impersonal pronouns, see Benveniste, p. 256.

A contradiction of this metaphor, however, resides in the rhetorical form, still a fragment of dialogue. The speaker can imagine himself a dead man, an immutable other. But the continuation of the "je"/"tu" relationship in the poem, which begins: "Sur ma face de mort on lira mes études," makes the reader aware that the text is an incomplete projection of the self into otherness. Although it is certain that death will give the lyrical I a state of permanence, in his present condition, the subject (even the Christian subject) cannot know what that mode will be:

> un horizontal présenté, reçu? mal reçu? expulsé?
> il entrera dans la nacrure?
> il restera dans la Saumure   (DP, p. 75)

Now that we have identified the interlocutors of Jacob's dialogism, we might consider classifying the variants in two groups: the dialogues (where the "tu" refers to God, Satan, or vocatives associated with either of these referents) and the monologues (where the "tu" alludes to the "je"). This would be possible, if it were not for the poems in which it cannot be determined whether the first and second persons are referentially distinct or identical. A number of texts, focussing on the inherent ambiguity or shifting nature of personal pronouns,[18] evoke dramatic opposition without specifying the antagonists. "Angoisses et autres," one of Jacob's most well known religious lyrics, whose harmonious versification is uncharacteristic of the poet, opens with an explicit address to the divine Other: "J'ai peur que Tu ne t'offenses." (B, p. 125) In the second stanza, however, the identity of the interlocutors is no longer certain, for the referents of the "je" and "tu" are not named. From the context, we may assume the "tu" refers to the speaker of the first stanza, the writer of the poem:

> Qu'écriras-tu en ces vers
> ou bien Dieu que tu déranges
> Dieu les prêtres et les anges
> ou bien tes amours d'enfer

---

[18] Personal pronouns belong to the class of signs (Jakobson's "shifters") whose referential meaning depends on their articulation in a given instance of speech. Cf. Roman Jakobson, *Essais de linguistique générale*, tr. Nicolas Ruwet (Paris: Editions de Minuit, 1963), p. 179; Benveniste, p. 252.

But can we be equally sure the implicit subject of these verses is the poet speaking to himself? Or is it, perhaps, the divine Other answering the opening invocation?

This ambivalence might be taken for a fortuitous technical oversight, if the pattern were not regularly repeated throughout Jacob's religious poetry. The following exchange occurs in a previously cited "Examen de conscience":

> Aveugle fou! Pourtant Dieu me fit grâce.
> Alors! Croyez-vous que je m'amendasse?
> De plus en plus lorsque Dieu t'avoisine
> de plus en plus le diable te résine.   (DP, p. 84)

The familiar second person may logically be identified as the penitent first person of the preceding couplet. But who speaks this exhortation? Again, does the speaker answer his own question, or does an unknown interlocutor (the "vous" of line two?) provide the response? These texts, in which the second person remains unidentified, afford a link between the "monologues" and "dialogues," almost an abstract model for the variants of Jacob's dialogism. In these instances, the dialogue with the self and the dialogue of the self and the other merge, the consciousness of duality is simultaneously introjected and projected. This movement represents a mystical aspiration, like the tendency of the "je" to be obliterated by God or Satan. The voice of the unknown interlocutor possesses a diffuse or ubiquitous subjectivity, located neither within nor outside of the "je."

In Jacob's writing, the dialectic embodied in the figure of dialogism has both psychological and metaphysical significations. Rhetorically, his poetry actualizes the alternation of self-assertion and self-obliteration fundamental to consciousness of the self. The "je" establishing its identity is always a "tu." No one, perhaps, has formulated this idea more concisely than Rimbaud: "JE est un autre." [19] Jacob effectively dramatized the experience in his poetry and even explicated the process in a poem called "Psychologie No. 2." The self-aware subject either conducts a monologue in front of his mirror:

---

[19] Rimbaud, *Œuvres*, p. 251.

> Regarde-toi dans cette glace qui déforme,
> va chez le photographe qu'il te donne une forme,
> fais ta toilette en chic, prête-toi des surnoms.[20]

Or a dialogue with imaginary listeners:

> Dites-moi, chers amis, que c'est moi qui vous aime....
> Enseignez-moi que je parle, que j'écoute, que je retiens.
> Donnez-moi avec moi-même des liens.

The appeal to others, then, is not proselytistic. Rather it is motivated by the desire to get in touch with oneself through others, by the need to corroborate the fact one is there. The pursuit of identity through self-objectivization is one meaning of dialogism within Jacob's texts. In "Psychologie No. 2," the poetic speaker proposes an interesting extension of this interpretation, that is, its application to the act of writing itself. Viewed as a dialogue, as a "je" / "tu" relationship like those concretized in the poems, the poet's discourse also becomes the means of self-projection and self-creation:

> J'écris pour me prouver que le temps gris s'écoule
> par rapport à moi seul, par rapport à la foule.
> J'écris pour que ce vêtement soit sur au moins un.
> Je pense pour qu'il y ait sur ce fauteuil quelqu'un.

Because its constant dialogism defines the self and the other in a mutual relation, Jacob's religious poetry does not infer achievement of a mystical union with God. In his life, the poet attempted the silent communion of mystics: "Il y a un monde de silence et de paisible bonheur. C'est là que l'Esprit converse avec l'Esprit, sans paroles, mais par la directe intuition."[21] But he believed writing destroyed direct intuition: "L'extériorisation détruit la vie intérieure." (See above, p. 62) The metaphysical intention of his poetry was to maintain contact with God, to perpetually recreate his presence through dialogue. After every movement of the speaker toward fusion with the divine Other, there is an inevitable separation: the "je" returns, the dialectical exchange recommences.

---

[20] *Philosophies,* 1ʳᵉ ann., No. 4 (1924), 375.
[21] Cited by Lagarde, p. 84.

This exchange with a metaphysical interlocutor is not without an affinity to the psychological signification of Jacob's dialogism. For if identity depends on alterity, the permanent image of the self is to be found in absolute otherness, that is, in God. The ultimate Photographer giving the lyrical I his form is Christ: "c'est ton image ô Photographe / que j'obtiens au Révélateur." (HC, p. 63) In a poetic vision of paradise, these themes, in fact, are explicitly connected. After death, it is a dialogue with the divine Other that finally exposes the speaker's definitive self:

> ... j'ai le cœur nu j'approche
> Et l'univers photographie mon cristallin
> Ah! quel soulagement: les deux mains dans les poches
> A l'indulgent seigneur parler de grand matin.   (HC, p. 107)

CONCLUSIONS

> Qui parmi nous n'est pas un *homo duplex?* ... Heureux l'auteur qui ne craint pas de se montrer en négligé! Et malgré l'humiliation éternelle que l'homme éprouve à se sentir confessé, heureux le lecteur pensif, l'*homo duplex,* qui, sachant reconnaître dans l'auteur son miroir, ne craint pas de s'écrier: *Thou art the man!* Voilà mon confesseur![1]

The revelation of universal duplicity was the purpose Baudelaire thus admired in *La Double vie,* a collection of short stories by Charles Asselineau. In praising the unreserved sincerity of the author's style, he compared the text to a personal letter or monologue. Baudelaire might have found the same qualities in the poetry of Max Jacob. Whether or not Jacob read these remarks of one of his nineteenth century paragons,[2] his spiritual, psychological, and aesthetic rapport with the Baudelairian concept of *homo duplex* is striking.

In an early prose poem of the *Œuvres burlesques et mystiques* (1912), Jacob exposed the principal aspects of the theme to be developed in his subsequent writings:

Le Double

> Chacun marche précédé de son double, reflet ... seule réalité, chacun marche ici-bas précédé de son double, peu semblable à l'original. Illusion, dites-vous? Les hommes ne sont pas si fous: le double, c'est nous. Que le double est paisible! Le double est d'une autre patrie que la terre, pourtant il est de la même patrie. Douce image, Marguerite

---

[1] Baudelaire, *Œuvres,* p. 662.
[2] Kamber's study discusses in detail Baudelairian themes in Jacob's works.

> du Faust, toi qui marches devant moi, t'invoquerai-je comme mon double? Hélas! tu n'es pas la seule ombre qui me précède: devant toi, devant nous... celui-ci... celui qui a pour sourire une ride! Horreur et désespoir du vent! Je ne veux aimer que toi, Marguerite! O Marguerite, aidez-moi à connaître mon double: toi! le vrai! pas l'autre, hélas! (SM/OBM, p. 257)

Every man is preceded not by one but by two doubles, who are positive and negative poles, like Marguerite and Faust, smiles and frowns, peacefulness and horrible despair, truth and its opposite. Dialectically, the division within the subject internalizes the oppositions of external reality ("le double, c'est nous"), while the cosmic oppositions ("d'une autre patrie que la terre"), reciprocally, project the self ("reflet," "ombre"). The desire of the lyrical I is for identification with one of these doubles: "aidez-moi à connaître mon double." And since the double is also the self, this desired capacity for recognition would confer an unequivocal identity on the subject. Yet, at the same time, the double, participating in both the natural and supernatural worlds, remains partially independent and beyond the control of the speaker, who hopes for outside assistance.

Max Jacob's fictional surrogates were double men. Victor Matorel of the novel *Saint Matorel* (1911) mounts to heaven on a horse, with Emile Cordier, his double, on its croupe. With *La Défense de Tartufe* (1919) Jacob appropriated the very archetype of *l'homme double*. It is revealing, too, that the *Miroir d'astrologie* (1949), written by the poet in collaboration with Conrad Moricand, listed duplicity first among the failings of persons born under Jacob's zodiacal sign. The accompanying horoscope for characters subjected to the influence of Cancer depicted a protean personality, whose self-image is an illusory reflection:

> La mobilité, l'instabilité. Ce sont des médiums. Ils n'ont pas une personnalité distincte. Ils en ont une quantité qu'ils s'approprient suivant les besoins et suivant les instants, mais qui ne leur appartient jamais en propre.
> Nature profondément suggestibles. Impressionnabilité excessive, sans contrôle. Plaque sensible sur laquelle tout vient se réfléchir. Natures passives, absorbantes. Ils sont changeants, capricieux, fluides, sans consistance. On ne les

saisit jamais. Ils donnent perpétuellement une illusion, aux autres comme à eux-mêmes. (pp. 73-74)

To this psychological profile, Jacob appended the confessory remark: "Ils sont poètes."

His own poetry was permeated with the theme of self-division. The *Cornet à dés* (1917) contains the following confession: "Je me suis tout donné à moi-même, pauvre paysan breton, le titre de duc, le droit de porter un monocle, j'ai pu grandir ma taille, ma pensée et je ne pourrai pas être digne de moi-même." (p. 53) With the repeated opposition of "je"/"moi-même," the subject become object, this line emphasizes the unbridgeable distance between consciousness of self and incarnations assumed in the world. In the poem "Mille regrets" of *Le Laboratoire central* (1921), an artist feels himself alienated from his past, a stranger in his native town:

> ... C'est l'amour
> De l'art qui m'a fait moi-même si lourd
> Que je ne pleure plus quand je traverse mon pays
> Je suis un inconnu: j'ai peur d'être haï. (p. 61)

While a penitent examining his conscience contemplates the Passion of Christ, in a text of *Fond de l'eau* (1927), his double (himself equipollent) sits forbodingly in hell:

> et mon double à son aise et fier
> parmi les plantes de l'enfer
> tout rehaussé de confessions
> mithridaté, mal reblanchi hétérodoxe
> équipollé par l'ergoterie sur l'orthodoxe
> une cave où les péchés parcheminés sont embaumés.
> (B, p. 147)

And, like "Le Double" of the *Œuvres burlesques et mystiques*, "Trop petit trop grand" of Jacob's posthumous collection *L'Homme de cristal* (1948), matches the subject's spiritual contradictions with moral and cosmic polarizations:

> Lequel de vous a vu mon âme
> quand elle reflète l'arc-en-ciel
> ô terre ô cieux je suis bigame
> Satan François d'Assise Ariel. (p. 103)

Throughout the present study we uncovered signs of Jacob's consciousness of duality not only among poetic motifs, but also in the shape of his ideas. Our introduction drew attention to the impression of rebirth at the moment of his first mystical revelation. Yet after baptism, Jacob felt the new man in himself at odds with the *vieux personnage* still inhabiting him, for the antithesis of sin and repentance continued to inform his existence. Within his religious beliefs, we observed the divergence of theosophy and faith. His desire for occult knowledge conflicted with the acceptance of Christian truths; his symbolical interpretations of the Old and New Testaments confuted the literal reading of the Bible consistent with Catholic orthodoxy. Jacob's writing on poetry reflected the contradictions of his metaphysics. Poetic theories defining the poem as an aesthetic object contradicted statements allowing poetry the function of mystical cognition. In descriptions of poetic execution, Jacob emphasized, alternatively, antithetical notions: style (technique) and situation (affectivity), interiorization (inspiration) and exteriorization (fabrication), maturation in the unconscious (automatism) and surveillance (conscious control). These contradictory theories matched his ambivalent attitude toward the relation of poetry and faith. At times, he stressed the compatibility and complementarity of the two domains; on occasion, he declared them irrevocably opposed.

Jacob's religious poetry embodied antitheses on several levels. Accompanying the *homo duplex* motif were the thematical oppositions of moral turpitude vs. remorse, demons vs. angels, damnation vs. salvation, earth vs. heaven, matter vs. spirit, the everyday vs. the mystical, the Kabbala vs. the Crucifixion, skepticism vs. faith, hypocrisy vs. sincerity. Structurally, an analogous pattern of stylistic contrasts predominated, with the counterpoint of burlesque, enigmatic, and confessional effects often concretizing the theoretical conflict of automatism and control. The rhetorical figure of dialogism reinforced themes of duplicity by constantly polarizing the first and second persons, to convey the sense of self-division and the parallel confrontation with the other, whose vocative field itself was split into two opposed categories.

To reduce these antithetical features to a single antagonism would betray their profusion and variety. To claim, for instance, bearing in mind Jacob's homosexuality, that the contrarieties of his writing signified the opposition of masculine and feminine. Or, given his moral and religious preoccupations, to interpret all oppositional signs as symbolic of the struggle of good and evil, that is, as a demonstration of manicheism. For, as engaged as he was in each of these conflicts, Jacob exhibited a more fundamental, or broader consciousness of duality, which constituted a view of man in the world. In elucidating the *homo duplex* motif, Baudelaire brought into relief the seemingly infinite dichotomies of life: "L'intention laissée en route, le rêve oublié dans une auberge, le projet barré par l'obstacle, le malheur et l'infirmité jaillissant du succès comme les plantes vénéneuses d'une terre grasse et négligée, le regret mêlé d'ironie, le regard jeté en arrière comme celui d'un vagabond qui se recueille un instant, l'incessant mécanisme de la vie terrestre, taquinant et déchirant à chaque minute l'étoffe de la vie idéale." [3] For Jacob, too, contradiction was not limited to a single conceptual antithesis; it was a psychological and ontological reality at the center of the human condition.

This incessant mechanism of duplicity might be looked at in two ways, either positively or negatively. In the preceding quotation, Baudelaire regrets its destruction of ideal wholeness. A similar nostalgia for unity emanates from instances of the theatrical metaphor in Jacob's writing, where role-playing usurps identity and undermines the reality of existence: "Acteur! il est acteur! et tous les jours à une brillante dame il déclare son amour. La dame est acteur; et acteur son amour." (DP, p. 108) The sense of inconsistency suggested by Jacob's figures of the double man, the actor, or the clown, frequently evoked anxiety. It was a mode of consciousness equivalent to Sartre's explication of the awareness of human freedom, which he exemplified by the dizziness of a man on the edge of a precipice. This dizziness is caused not by fear of accidentally slipping, but by the anguish inherent in the possibility of choosing to throw oneself into the abyss. [4] Jacob, similarly, was afraid of sinful temptations, but felt anguish at the knowledge of his freedom to sin, at the distance between intention and act. For, as Sartre explained in *L'Etre et le néant*, the dichotomy of our present and future selves corrodes identity: "*Je suis celui que je*

---

[3] *Œuvres*, p. 658.
[4] Jean-Paul Sartre, *L'Etre et le néant*, pp. 67-69.

serai sur le mode de ne l'être pas.... C'est précisément la conscience d'être son propre avenir sur le mode du n'être-pas que nous nommerons *l'angoisse.*"[5] In analyzing Jacob's dialogism, with its perpetual projection of the subject as an other and constant appeal to an absolute Other, we discovered a similar consciousness of nothingness — *Je suis... le double zéro* (HC, p. 46) — and the concomitant desire for stability, for unity, for an end to freedom, for death.

Yet, the poet sometimes welcomed the duplicity essential to self-affirmation and change. If second person exhortations condemned the past incarnations of the lyrical I, first person confessions and supplications hopefully projected a transformed future self. And in a defense of Tartufe, Jacob reversed the metaphorical significance of the actor's mask, to convey, instead of inauthenticity, the sincerity of a man striving toward spiritual perfection: "C'est ici la clef du Tartuffe. L'habit ne fait pas le moine! voilà un dicton qui dans un sens différent de l'ordinaire ne mérite plus d'être en proverbe. 'Allez à l'église de force pour un jour le faire de gré', dit à peu près Pascal, et Tartuffe sait bien qu'on devient moine sous l'habit comme dévot à la messe." (DT, p. 295) The same association of "virtue" and the "theatrical sense" was made by Yeats, in his *Autobiography*: "If we cannot imagine ourselves as different from what we are and assume that second self, we cannot impose a discipline upon ourselves, though we may accept one from others. Active virtue as distinguished from the passive acceptance of a current code is therefore theatrical, consciously dramatic, the wearing of a mask."[6] What these poets both understood was the relation of self-division to moral action and creativity.

Confession was the mode chosen by Max Jacob to transcend duality, and the mirrors in which he sought his undivided image were prayer and poetry. There was more than a hint of truth in his claim to have acquired all his knowledge from Rousseau "dont les *Confessions* m'apprirent à lire quand j'avais dix ans et m'ont appris tout depuis." (*Corr.*, II, 102) For Jacob shared with Rousseau the intention of self-revelation, as intimated by the name of

---

[5] *Ibid.*, p. 69.
[6] *The Autobiography of W. B. Yeats* (New York: MacMillan, 1938), pp. 400-401.

his last collection of poems, *L'Homme de cristal,* which might have been inspired by the *Confessions*: "On a vu, dans tout le cours de ma vie, que mon cœur, transparent comme le cristal, n'a jamais su cacher durant une minute entière un sentiment un peu vif qui s'y fut réfugié." [7] But the desire of these writers for absolute transparency demanded they reveal their own vacillations, contradictions, and doubts. So the lyrical I of the title poem "L'Homme de cristal" is painfully divided:

> Le Paradis a ses respirations
> le long du dos en travers de vertèbres.
> Voici mes pieds! les plantes en pente
> pour mieux glisser dans le feu des Ténèbres.
>
> (HC, p. 13)

Like devotional confessions, Jacob's religious poetry dramatized a quest for salvation, or wholeness, through the avowal of duplicity. And these poems, paradoxically, derived unity from their multiform exhibition of the double man.

---

[7] Jean-Jacques Rousseau, *Œuvres complètes,* Bibliothèque de la Pléiade (Paris: Gallimard, 1959), I, 446. To achieve transparency was the purpose Rousseau explicitly assigned to his *Confessions,* at the end of the *Livre Quatrième,* I, p. 175: "Je voudrais pouvoir en quelque façon rendre mon âme transparente aux yeux du lecteur, et pour cela je cherche à la lui montrer sous tous les points de vue, à l'éclairer par tous les jours, à faire en sorte qu'il ne s'y passe pas un mouvement qu'il n'aperçoive, afin qu'il puisse juger par lui-même du principe qui les produit." Although *L'Homme de cristal* was published posthumously, its editors note that Jacob himself had grouped a number of texts under that title.

APPENDIX

MAX JACOB AND THE SURREALISTS

The preceding study referred to several instances of Max Jacob's interconnection with the Surrealist movement. Chapter II discussed points of convergence and divergence in their respective theories on the function of the unconscious in poetic execution. My analysis of stylistic tendencies, in Chapter III, mentioned the similarity of Surrealist automatic writing to Jacob's burlesque and enigmatic effects characteristic not only of the *Cornet à dés* but also of his later poetry. Meanwhile, Tatiana Greene's well-documented article, "Max Jacob et le surréalisme," *French Forum*, 1 (Sept. 1976), 251-67, has clarified many details concerning the relationship, both personal and artistic, between Jacob and the Surrealists.

Certain mysteries, nevertheless, remain in the uncharted zones of biography. In my Preface, I tentatively accounted for the general neglect of Jacob's later poems written primarily in the religious or confessional mode by the fact that the Surrealists had begun to ignore him. In 1916, he had collaborated on small reviews, alongside Breton, Aragon, and Soupault, as Maurice Nadeau's *Histoire du surréalisme* records: "Ecrivaient également à *Nord-Sud*: Apollinaire, Max Jacob, dont les noms voisinent avec ceux de Breton, Aragon, Soupault."[1] Jacob also contributed to *Littérature,* whose directors were the same three poets, soon to become the founders of Surrealism.[2] Yet something may have occurred (perhaps, the older poet's retreat to Saint-Benoît?) to prevent Breton from includ-

---

[1] (Paris: Editions du Seuil, 1964), p. 20.
[2] *Ibid.*, p. 31.

ing the name of Max Jacob in his *Manifeste du surréalisme* (1924). This omission, which could only have been deliberate, implies a motive beyond aesthetics. For although there were differences between Jacob's and the Surrealists' views on poetry, Breton did refer to other predecessors who displayed Surrealistic tendencies in some but not all features of their writing. Even while paying homage to Apollinaire, the manifesto underscored his refusal to sacrifice certain "médiocres moyens littéraires."[3] Like Professor Greene, I wonder why Breton, who called Baudelaire "surréaliste dans la morale," and Jarry "surréaliste dans l'absinthe,"[4] did not accord Jacob the epithet: *surréaliste dans la religion*.

Having encountered a number of Max Jacob's revealing comments on the Surrealists, diffused in various sources, I decided their assemblage might be useful to readers. These antagonistic yet often humorous remarks delineate his bitter sense of abandonment by the successful young poets, his resentment at not having received due credit as their precursor, and the bearing of his religious beliefs on their discord. The following citations come from his correspondence, except for the extract from "Le Tiers transporté, Chronique des temps héroïques," a memoir of artistic activity on Montmartre, written by Jacob for *Les Feux de Paris* in 1937. The renunciation of Surrealist techniques, cited in Chapter II (see above, p. 56), appeared in a letter of October 20, 1939, to Pierre Andreu.

---

[3] André Breton, *Manifestes du surréalisme* (Paris: Editions du Sagittaire, 1946), p. 43.
[4] *Ibid.*, p. 47.

A. 1924-1926:

>A Marcel Jouhandeau
>Saint-Benoît-sur-Loire
>12 octobre 1924

J'ai eu bien de l'aigreur ces jours-ci à propos du surréalisme. On étale les hallucinations de l'œil, de l'ouïe de M. André Breton, en travail, en demi-sommeil et autres calembours mystiques, j'ai passé ma vie à travailler ainsi, et c'est lui qui a le bénéfice de cette découverte pour l'avoir décorée d'un mot qui est d'Apollinaire... Et personne ne dit rien, on l'encense et moi dans mon coin je deviens de plus en plus obscur et méprisé de la jeunesse. (*Corr.*, II, 335)

>A Jules Supervielle
>24 juillet 1925
>St.-Benoît

Les surréalistes me font rire. On va revenir à une littérature d'émotion directe: la gaieté, la jeunesse et l'amour ou les caractères étudiés. Les surréalistes en feront un nez! Il n'y a là-dedans qu'un homme *natif* c'est le pauvre Tzara. Quant à Artaud, s'il avait vécu il y a soixante ans, il serait baptisé "génie" depuis sept ans. Il ne parle que de ses cheveux et il a raison — il parle aussi de son ventre — il a tout. (MS 23g4 2/2, Jacques Doucet Collection, Paris)

>A Jean Cocteau
>17 rue Gabrielle 1926

Ma lettre devrait être remise 20 jours avant la parution du numéro, me dit Aragon. Je crois "Littérature" de nos amis (??) — Je doute de tout. (*Choix de lettres de Max Jacob à Jean Cocteau, 1919-1944* [Paris: P. Morihien, 1949], p. 22)

A Jean Cocteau
21 février 1926

J'ai reçu sans raison, brusquement, une lettre d'*effroyables* injures d'André Breton. Je n'ai pas répondu. (*Ibid.*, p. 34)

A Jean Cocteau
14 mars 1926
St.-Benoît-la-Pioche,
Loiret

Le même docteur lit chez moi la "Révolution Surréaliste" qu'on m'envoie sans doute pour me narguer, pour que j'y trouve mes calembours musicaux signés par d'autres.... Les surréalistes n'ont pas assez de foi pour être des magiciens. Encore faudrait-il qu'ils croient aux démons et aux anges.... Cette rage contre Dieu à toutes les lignes prouve qu'ils sont, eux, possédés du démon, c'est le signe caractéristique de la possession que les injures à Dieu auxquelles un homme normal ne pense même pas. (*Ibid.*, pp. 40-41)

B. 1937-1940:

Alors pas la suite surréaliste! Quel dommage! D'ailleurs n'auront l'honneur de mon attention que ceux qui m'ont fait celui de la leur avec bienveillance. A ceux qui m'ont seulement prêtée leur attention, je ne la rendrai pas. Pas les surréalistes, puisqu'ils ignorent mon nom bien qu'ils connaissent assez mes œuvres ... pour pouvoir les ignorer. ("Le Tiers transporté, Chronique des temps héroïques," *Les Feux de Paris*, Nos. 7-8 [jan. 1937], n. pag.)

A René-Guy Cadou

Je prends X pour un *blagueur*, ainsi que tous les surréalistes: ils s'amusent, c'est bien. Ils amusent les autres, c'est mieux, mais la poésie c'est Lorca ou Kafka. Il y a plus de poésie dans le sincère Salmon ou dans Milosz que dans aucun surréaliste. (*Esth.*, p. 48)

A Marcel Béalu
28 mars 1940

Les artistes ne sont pas des hommes mais des monstres presque toujours, bêtes presque toujours. Dans les grandes époques, les artistes étaient des hommes, et parfois des hommes supérieurs aux autres. Le charlatanisme surréaliste vient d'être démasqué! M. Aragon, auteur d'un traité sur le style, publie un roman dans la N.R.F. C'est tout juste comme un mauvais candidat au prix Goncourt. Bien la peine de casser des tables de café pour aboutir à ça! (*Lettres*, pp. 187-188)

SELECTED BIBLIOGRAPHY

I. BIBLIOGRAPHIES

For additional bibliographies of works by and about Max Jacob, see, Billy, *Max Jacob*; Henry, "Bio-bibliographie de Max Jacob"; Kamber, *Max Jacob and the Poetics of Cubism*; Pfau, *Zur antinomie der bürgerlichen satire; untersuchungen über leben und werk Max Jacobs*; Plantier, *Max Jacob*; St. Thomas, "Les éléments du comique dans l'œuvre de Max Jacob"; Schneider, "The Poetic Theories and the Poetry of Max Jacob"; Thau, *Poetry and Antipoetry; A Study of Selected Aspects of Max Jacob's Poetic Style* (full references cited below). See also John Stanley Collier, ed., *Max Jacob, Lettres, 1920-1941: à T. Briant et C. Valence* (Oxford: Basil Blackwell, 1966); Max Jacob, *Histoire du roi Kaboul 1er et du marmiton Gauwain*, Les Cahiers Max Jacob, No. 1 (Paris: Les Amis de Max Jacob, 1951) and *Lettres imaginaires*, Les Cahiers Max Jacob, No. 2 (Paris: Les Amis de Max Jacob, 1952); Jean de Palacio, "Bibliographie sélective des origines à 1970," RLM, Nos. 336-339 (1973), 192-205; Peter C. Hoy, "Carnet bibliographique 1971-1972," RLM, Nos. 474-478 (1976), 191-199.

The following list of references is a guide to criticism on Max Jacob.

II. BOOKS ON MAX JACOB

Andreu, Pierre. *Max Jacob*. ("Conversions Célèbres.") Paris: Wesmael-Charlier, 1962.
Béalu, Marcel. *Dernier visage de Max Jacob*. Followed by *Lettres à Marcel Béalu* by Max Jacob. Lyon: Emmanuel Vitte, 1959.
Belaval, Yvon. *La Rencontre avec Max Jacob*. Paris: Charlot, 1946.
Billy, André. *Max Jacob*. Rev. ed. ("Poètes d'aujourd'hui," No. 3.) Paris: Pierre Seghers, 1945.
Emié, Louis. *Dialogues avec Max Jacob*. ("Mises au point.") Paris: Corréa, Buchet et Chastel, 1954.
Fabureau, Hubert. *Max Jacob: son œuvre*. ("Collection des Célébrités Contemporaines," 3rd ser., No. 3.) Paris: Editions de la Nouvelle revue critique, 1935.
Jannini, Pasquale Aniel. *L'esprit nouveau e le poetiche di Max Jacob*. Milano: Editrice Viscontea, 1966. New edition with change of title: *L'angelo funambolo; Le poetiche di Max Jacob*. Milano: Istituto Editoriale Cisalpino-La Goliardica, 1973.

Kamber, Gerald. *Max Jacob and the Poetics of Cubism.* Baltimore and London: The Johns Hopkins Press, 1971.

Lagarde, Pierre. *Max Jacob, mystique et martyr, avec trente-deux méditations inédites, cinq poèmes, deux autographes, un dessin, par Max Jacob, et un profil du poète par Serge.* Paris: Editions Baudinière, 1944.

Parturier, Maurice. *Max Jacob: Notes biographiques.* Paris: Le Divan, 1944.

Pérard, Joseph. *Max Jacob l'universel.* Colmar: Editions Alsatia, 1974.

Pfau, Una. *Zur antinomie der bürgerlichen satire; untersuchungen über leben und werk Max Jacobs.* ("Europäische Hochschulschriften," Reihe xiii, "Französische Sprache und Literatur") Bern: Herbert Lang; Frankfurt: Peter Lang, 1975.

Plantier, René. *Max Jacob.* ("Les Ecrivains devant Dieu.") Paris: Desclée de Brouwer, 1972.

Rousselot, Jean. *Max Jacob, l'homme qui faisait penser à Dieu.* Paris: Laffont, 1946.

———. *Max Jacob au serieux.* Rodez: Editions Subervie, 1958.

Salmon, André. *Max Jacob: Poète, peintre, mystique et homme de qualité.* Paris: René Girard, 1927.

Thau, Annette. *Poetry and Antipoetry; A Study of Selected Aspects of Max Jacob's Poetic Style.* ("North Carolina Studies in the Romance Languages and Literatures," Essays, Number 5) Chapel Hill: University of North Carolina, Department of Romance Languages, 1976.

Wyss, Tobias. *Dialog und stille; Max Jacob, Giuseppe Ungaretti, Fernando Pessoa.* Zürich: Juris Druck, 1969.

III. OTHER WORKS (Articles, Chapters, Dissertations, Prefaces) ON MAX JACOB

Albert-Birot, Pierre. "Note liminaire." *L'Homme de cristal.* By Max Jacob. Paris: Gallimard, 1967, pp. 9-12.

Allard, Roger. "Le Laboratoire central, Dos d'Arlequin." NRF, 17 (déc., 1921), 743-746.

Andreu, Pierre. "Max Jacob romancier." RLM, Nos. 474-478 (1976), 23-34.

Antoine, Gérald. "Max Jacob: Une Doctrine littéraire." *F Monde,* 53 (1967), 16-21.

Apollinaire, Guillaume. "La Phalange nouvelle." *La Poésie symboliste.* By Guillaume Apollinaire, V-E. Michelet, and P. M. Roinard. Paris: "L'Edition," 1909, p. 180.

Arland, Marcel. "L'Homme de chair et l'homme reflet." NRF, 22 (juin, 1924), 747-48.

———. "Le Terrain Bouchabelle." NRF, 23 (août, 1923), 228-30.

———. "Visions infernales." NRF, 23 (sept., 1924), 360.

"Autour de Max Jacob." *Philobiblion: Bulletin périodique de beaux libres,* No. 72 (1938), 29-41.

Béalu, Marcel. "Max Jacob, poète." *Cahiers du Nord,* 22e ann., Nos. 3-4 (avr., 1951), 196-204.

Béguin, Albert. "Destin de Max Jacob." *Poésie de la présence.* ("Les Cahiers du Rhône," 95.) Neuchâtel: La Baconnière, 1957, pp. 275-283.

Belaval, Yvon. "Le Laboratoire central." NRF, 15, Nos. 86 and 88 (1960), 295-305; 734-44.

———. "Préface." *Le Laboratoire central.* By Max Jacob. Paris: Gallimard, 1960, pp. 9-41.

Berger, Pierre. "Pour un portrait de Max Jacob." *Europe*, 36, Nos. 348-49 (avr.-mai, 1958), 56-73.
Billy, André. "Max Jacob." *Huysmans et Cie.* Paris: Nizet, 1962, pp. 195-227.
Blanchet, André. "La Conversion de Max Jacob." *La Littérature et le spirituel.* ("La mêlée littéraire," vol. I) Paris: Editions Montaigne, 1959, pp. 13-83.
―――. "Introduction." *La Défense de Tartufe.* By Max Jacob. Paris: Gallimard, 1964, pp. 13-67.
Boschère, Jean de. "Une lettre de Jean de Boschère." *France-Asie*, 3 (avr., 1948), 520-29.
Bounoure, Gabriel. "*Les Pénitents en maillots roses: Visions infernales; Fond de l'eau; Rivages*, par Max Jacob." NRF, 43, No. 250 (juill.-déc., 1934), 109-118.
Bouret, Jean. "Deux Rétrospectives: Max Jacob et Guillaumin." *Les Lettres françaises*, No. 26 (oct., 1944).
Brenner, Jacques. "Le Cornet acoustique." RLM, Nos. 474-478 (1976), 11-17.
Breunig, Leroy C. "Max Jacob et Picasso." *Mercure de France*, 131 (déc., 1957), 581-96.
Brezu-Stoian, Constandina. "Max Jacob en Roumanie." RLM, Nos. 474-478 (1976), 117-144.
Brissaud, André. "Préface." *Correspondance de Max Jacob.* Ed. François Garnier. Paris: Editions de Paris, 1953, I, pp. I-XIX.
Cadou, René-Guy. "L'Œuvre de Max Jacob." *Cahiers du Nord*, 22ᵉ ann., Nos. 3-4 (avr., 1951), 178-95.
Carco, Francis. No title. *Aguedal*, 4ᵉ ann., No. 2, "Hommage à Max Jacob" (mai, 1939), 148.
Cassou, Jean. "Max Jacob et la liberté." NRF, 30 (avr., 1928), 455-63.
―――. "Adieu à Max Jacob." *Cahiers du Sud*, No. 273 (2ᵉ semestre, 1945), 561-64.
Cattaui, Georges. "Max Jacob est mort il y a vingt-cinq ans." RdP, 76 (juin, 1969), 143-45.
Caws, Mary Ann. "Jacobean Structures and a Few Signs." *Folio*, No. 9 (Oct. 1976), 15-18.
Cingria, Charles-Albert. "Image de Max Jacob." *Aguedal*, 4ᵉ ann., No. 2, "Hommage à Max Jacob" (mai, 1939), 151-54.
Charensol, G. "Comment écrivez-vous? enquête." *Nouvelles Littéraires*, ann. 11 (fév., 1932), 5.
Claudel, Paul. "Lettre à Max Jacob à propos des *Morceaux choisis*." *Aguedal*, 4ᵉ ann., No. 2 (mai, 1939), 102.
Cocteau, Jean. "Max Jacob." *Le Disque vert*, 2ᵉ ann., No. 2, "En hommage à Max Jacob" (nov., 1923), 30-31.
―――. "Mathématicien, mais de rêve." *Europe*, 36, Nos. 348-49 (avr.-mai, 1958), 3.
Collier, Stanley John. "The Correspondence of Max Jacob." FS, 7, No. 3 (July, 1953), 235-56.
―――. "Max Jacob and the *poème en prose*." MLR, 51, No. 4 (Oct., 1956), 522-35.
―――. "Max Jacob's *Le Cornet à dés*: A Critical Analysis." FS, 11 (1957), 149-167.
Crémieux, Benjamin. "Max Jacob et le poème en prose." *Le Disque vert*, 2ᵉ ann., No. 2 (nov., 1923), 13-15.
Délétang-Tardif, Yanette. "La Mort d'un poète." *Poésie 44*, 5ᵉ ann., No. 20 (juill.-oct., 1944), 40-42.

Delteil, Joseph. "Max Jacob et le poème en prose." *Le Disque vert*, 2ᵉ ann., No. 2 (nov., 1923), 59.

———. No title. *Aguedal*, 4ᵉ ann., No. 2 "Hommage à Max Jacob" (mai, 1939), 156.

Desse, Georges. "Laissé pour conte." *Les Cahiers de l'Iroise*, 9ᵉ ann. (juill.-sept., 1962).

Dion Henri. "Max Jacob au carrefour de la douleur et de l'amour." *Renaissance de Fleury*, No. 54 (juill., 1965), 4-6.

Duhamel, Georges. "Les Poèmes." MF, 103, No. 384 (juin, 1913), 800.

Emile-Blanche, Jacques. "Le Multiple Génie de Max Jacob." *Le Disque vert*, 2ᵉ ann., No. 2 (nov., 1923), 32-34.

Fargue, Léon-Paul. *Portraits de famille: Souvenirs*. Paris: J. B. Janin, 1947, pp. 195-208.

Fels, Fernand. "Max Jacob, peintre d'images." *Le Disque vert*, 2ᵉ ann., No. 2 (nov., 1923), 26-29.

Fierens, Paul. "Max Jacob, poète catholique." *Le Disque vert*, 2ᵉ ann., No. 2 (nov., 1923), 23-25.

Florens, Paul. "La Poésie de Max Jacob," *Le Mail*, No. 5 (avr., 1928), 232-36.

Fontainas, André. "Le Laboratoire central." MR, 149 (août, 1921), 739-40.

———. "Les Pénitents en maillots roses." MF, 186 (juin 1926), 671-72.

Fowlie, Wallace. "Hommage to Max Jacob." *Poetry*, 75, No. 6 (March, 1950), 352-356.

———. "Max Jacob: The Violence of the Supernatural." *Climate of Violence*. New York: The Macmillan Co., 1967, pp. 188-202.

Frick, Louis de Gonzague. "M. Max Jacob et le 'Cornet à dés.'" *SIC* No. 24 (déc., 1917), n. p.

Gabory, Georges. "Le Roi de Béotie." NRF, 38 (mars, 1922), 347-48.

Gandon, Yves. *Imageries critiques*. Paris: Société française d'éditions littéraires et techniques, 1933, 61-70.

Ganzo, Robert. *Cinq poètes assassinés: St. Pol Roux, Max Jacob, Robert Desnos, Benjamin Fondane et André Chennevières*. Paris: Editions de Minuit, 1948.

Garnier, François. "Max Jacob et le théâtre." *Europe*, Nos. 348-49 (avr.-mai, 1958), 37-45.

Ghéon, Henri. "La Défense de Tartufe." NRF, 7ᵉ ann., No. 78 (mars, 1920), 452-53.

Gide, André. "Max Jacob." *Aguedal*, 4ᵉ ann., No. 2, "Hommage à Max Jacob" (mai, 1939), 101.

Gourmont, Jean de. "Le Cinématoma." MF, 141, No. 529 (juill., 1920), 182.

Greene, Tatiana. "Max Jacob et le surréalisme." *French Forum*, 1 (Sept., 1976), 251-267.

Grenier, Jean. "Max Jacob." *Aguedal*, 4ᵉ ann., No. 2 (mai, 1939), 131-34.

———. "L'Art poétique de Max Jacob." *Combat* (nov., 1944), 6.

Guégen, Pierre. "Rivage." *Nouvelles littéraires*, ann. 11 (avr., 1932), 5.

Guiette, Robert. "Notes pour un portrait." *Le Disque vert*, 2ᵉ ann., No. 2 (nov., 1923), 52-53.

———. "Vie de Max Jacob." NRF, 43 (juill., 1934), 5-19; (août, 1934), 248-59.

Guillaume, Louis. "Max nous parle." *France-Asie*, 3 (mars, 1948), 364-68.

Guilloux, Louis. "Max Jacob." *France-Asie*, 3 (mars, 1948), 351-63.

Harris, G. T. "André Malraux et l'Esthétique de Max Jacob." MLR, 66, No. 3 (July, 1971), 565-67.

Henry, Hélène. "Bio-bibliographie de Max Jacob." *Europe*, 36, Nos. 348-49 (avr.-mai, 1958), 110-20.

———. "Max Jacob et la Bretagne." *Europe*, 36, Nos. 348-49 (avr.-mai, 1958), 7-18.

———. "Max Jacob et Quimper." *Les Cahiers de l'Iroise*, 9ᵉ ann. (juill.-sept., 1962), 131-37.

———. "Guillaume et Max." *Europe*, 44, Nos. 451-52 (1966), 124-32.

———. "Max Jacob et Picasso: Jalons chronologiques pour une amitié, 1901-1944." *Europe*, Nos. 492-93 (avr.-mai, 1970), 191-210.

Hertz, Henri. "La Côte." *Phalange*, 7ᵉ ann. (avr., 1912), 329-32.

———. "Avec Max Jacob, en compagnie de la renommée." *Le Disque vert*, 2ᵉ ann., No. 2, "En hommage à Max Jacob" (nov., 1923), 21.

———. "Sur une vie, sur un art, les fines empreintes des nouvelles merveilles de la science." *Europe*, 36, Nos. 348-49 (avr.-mai, 1958), 18-26.

"L'homme de chair et l'homme reflet." *Almanach des lettres françaises et étrangères*, 1ʳᵉ ann. (avr.-mai-juin, 1924), 91.

Hubert, Renée Riese. "Max Jacob: The Poetics of *Le Cornet à dés*." *About French Poetry From Dada to "Tel Quel": Text and Theory*. Ed. by Mary Ann Caws. Detroit: Wayne State Univ. Press, 1974, 99-111.

———. "Max Jacob's Bourgeois Voices." *Folio*, No. 9 (Oct., 1976), 38-42.

Jouhandeau, Marcel. "Max Jacob et Supervielle à Guéret." *Bon an, mal an, 1908-1928; Mémorial VII*. Paris: Gallimard, 1972, 185-92.

Kamber, Gerald. "Max Jacob et Charles Baudelaire: Une étude de sources." MLN, 78 (May, 1963), 252-60.

———. "André Gide and Max Jacob." *Folio*, No. 9 (Oct., 1976), 43-46.

Lannes, Roger. "Hommage à Max Jacob." *Aguedal*, 4ᵉ ann., No. 2, "Hommage à Max Jacob" (mai, 1939), 161-62.

———. "Max Jacob." *Poésie 44*, No. 20 (juill.-oct., 1944), 35-39.

———. "Max Jacob commenté par lui-même." *Arts*, No. 1 (jan., 1945), 3.

———. "Préface." *Morven le Gaëlique*. By Max Jacob. Paris: Gallimard, 1953, pp. 9-13.

Larnac, Jean. "Un Curieux mystique." *Le Divan*, No. 252 (oct.-déc., 1944), 392-94.

Le Bot, Marc. "Max Jacob, esthéticien?" *Europe*, 36, Nos. 348-49 (avr.-mai, 1958), 46-56.

Le Dantec, Yves Gérard. "Max Jacob et la muse celtique." *Le Mail*, No. 5 (avr., 1928), 264-66.

Leiris, Michel. "Préface." *Le Cornet à dés*. By Max Jacob. ("Collection Poésie.") Paris: Gallimard, 1967, pp. 8-13.

———. "Saint Matorel martyr." *Brisées*. Paris: Mercure de France, 1966, pp. 82-90.

Levanti, Michel. "La Vie et l'œuvre de Max Jacob." *Aguedal*, 4ᵉ ann., No. 2, "Hommage à Max Jacob" (mai, 1939), 103-13.

Lévy, Sydney S. "Une poétique du jeu: Etude sur *Le Cornet à dés* de Max Jacob." DAI, 32 (1971), 440A.

———. "Que faire de Max Jacob?" *Sub-stance*, No. zéro (1971), 31-37.

———. "Jeu et poésie: Une lecture du *Cornet à dés* de Max Jacob." *Sub-stance*, No. 4 (1972), 27-44.

———. "The Poetry of Diversion." *Folio*, No. 9 (Oct., 1976), 5-14.

Livet, Henri Philippe. "Hommage à Max Jacob." *Aguedal*, 4ᵉ ann., No. 2 (mai, 1939), 163-64.

Lockerbie, S. I. "Realism and fantasy in the work of Max Jacob; Some verse poems." *Order and adventure in Post-Romantic French Poetry.* Essays presented to C. A. Hackett. Ed. by E. M. Beaumont, J. M. Cocking and J. Cruickshank. Oxford: Basil Blackwell, 1973, pp. 149-61.

Magny, Olivier de. "Le Laboratoire central, par Max Jacob." *Les Lettres françaises,* 8ᵉ ann., No. 7 (oct., 1960), 179-80.

Malraux, André. "Art poétique, par Max Jacob." NRF, 19 (août, 1922), 227-28.

Manoll, Michell. "La Part de Dieu." *Aguedal,* 4.ᵉ ann., No. 2, "Hommage à Max Jacob" (mai, 1939), 180-81.

Mauriac, Claude. "Les Vies parallèles de Max Jacob." *Preuves,* 4, No. 35 (janv., 1954), 80-83.

Méral, Paul. "La Méthode de Max Jacob." *Le Disque vert,* 2ᵉ ann., No. 2 (nov., 1923), 552-53.

Oberlé, Jean. "Max Jacob, poète et martyr." *La France Libre,* No. 44 (juin, 1944), 102-04.

Oxenhandler, Neal. "Jacob's Struggle with the Angel." YFS, 12 (Fall/Winter, 1953), 41-66.

———. "Max Jacob and *Les Feux de Paris.*" UCPMP, 35, No. 4 (1964), 221-308.

———. "Concealed emotions in the poetry of Max Jacob." *Dada/Surrealism,* No. 5 (1975), 53-57.

Palacio, Jean de. "Un Précurseur inattendu de Max Jacob: Lord Byron." RLC, 45ᵉ ann., No. 2 (avr.-juin, 1971), 187-207.

———. "La Postérité du *Gaspard de la Nuit*: de Baudelaire à Max Jacob. RLM, Nos. 336-339 (1973), 157-189.

———. "Le sang et la crucifixion; Max Jacob d'après ses variantes, ou la passion de l'écrivain." RSH, 35 (1970), 593-601.

———. "La Publication du *Terrain Bouchaballe,* ou Max Jacob chez les Canaques." RLM, Nos. 474-478 (1976), 57-75.

———. "Un Roman inédit de Max Jacob: 'Les Gants blancs'." RLM, Nos. 474-478 (1976), 77-102.

Parrot, Louis. "Pur comme un Enfant, le souvenir de Max Jacob." *Les Lettres françaises,* No. 45 (mars, 1945), 1.

Parturier, Maurice. "Max Jacob." *Le Divan,* No. 252 (oct.-déc., 1944), 394-395.

"Le pauvre Max." *The Times Literary Supplement,* 9 Oct. 1959, p. 576.

Pelletier, Christian. "Max Jacob, Un regard sur la vie quotidienne vers 1920." Thèse pour le Doctorat de troisième cycle, Sorbonne, 1972.

———. "Le manuscrit du *Cornet à dés* de Max Jacob." IL, No. 5 (nov.-déc., 1974), 226-28.

———. "*Le Terrain Bouchaballe:* de la comédie au roman." RLM, Nos. 474-478 (1976), 35-56.

Petit, Paul. "Réponse à Max Jacob." *Aguedal,* 4ᵉ ann., No. 2 (mai, 1939), 134-38.

Pia, Pascal. "Filibuth." NRF, 22 (mai, 1923), 833-35.

———. "Etudes jacobiennes." *Carrefour,* No. 1018 (mars, 1964), 20.

Pinguet, Maurice. "L'Ecriture du rêve dans *Le Cornet à dés.*" RLM, Nos. 336-339 (1973), 13-52.

Plantier, René. "Présentation des textes." *Méditations.* By Max Jacob. Paris: Gallimard, 1972, pp. 7-45.

———. "La mythologie dans l'œuvre de Max Jacob," RLM, Nos. 336-339 (1973), 53-123.

Plantier, René. "Le Système poétique de Max Jacob." Première thèse pour le Doctorat ès-lettres, Sorbonne, 1973.
Porel, Jacques. "Le Cabinet noir." *Les Feuilles libres,* 4ᵉ ann., No. 28 (août-sept., 1922), 295-96.
———. "Le Rire de Max Jacob." *Le Disque vert,* 2ᵉ ann., No. 2 (nov., 1923), 35.
Raval, Maurice. "Le Coup de dés chez Jacob." *Le Disque vert,* 2ᵉ ann., No. 2 (nov., 1923), 50-51.
———. "A Propos de certaines curiosités esthétiques et critiques." *Les Feuilles libres,* 4ᵉ ann., No. 28 (août-sept., 1922), 295.
Romains, Jules. "Max Jacob." RDM, No. 10 (oct., 1970), 13-18. Also in his: *Amitiés et rencontres.* Paris: Flammarion, 1970, pp. 80-87.
Rose, Marilyn Gaddis. "Max Jacob's Referential Strategies: Space Manipulation in *Le Cornet à dés.*" *Folio,* No. 9 (Oct., 1976), 1-4.
Rousselot, Jean. "Max Jacob." *Cahiers du Nord,* 22ᵉ ann., Nos. 3-4 (avr., 1951), 205-10.
———. "Contribution à une esthétique de Max Jacob." *Revue d'esthétique,* 10 (juill.-sept., 1957), 296-318.
———. "Max Jacob ou le sel dans la plaie." *Présences contemporaines: Rencontres sur le chemin de la poésie.* Paris: Nouvelles Editions Debresse, 1958, pp. 127-140.
———. "Poète et martyr." *Les Nouvelles littéraires,* 42ᵉ ann., No. 1906 (mars, 1946), 2.
Rouzet, Georges. "Lettre de Max Jacob sur Julien Leclerq." *Vivre,* 4ᵉ ann. (avr., 1939), 6-7.
Roy, Claude. "Préface." *Ballades.* By Max Jacob. Paris: Gallimard, 1970, pp. 7-12.
Saint Thomas, Grâce Marie. "Les Eléments du comique dans l'œuvre de Max Jacob." Diss. Sorbonne, 1968.
Salmon, André. "L'Homme." *Le Disque vert,* 2ᵉ ann., No. 2, "En hommage à Max Jacob" (nov., 1923), 11.
———. "Cinq-Mars," *France-Asie,* 3 (mars, 1948), 353-56.
———. "Note liminaire." *Le Cornet à dés II.* By Max Jacob. Paris: Gallimard, 1955.
Sauguet, Henri. "Max Jacob et la musique." *Revue Musicale,* No. 210 (janv., 1952), 151-54.
Schneider, Judith M. "The Poetic Theories and the Poetry of Max Jacob." DAI, 31 (1970), 2401-02A.
———. "Max Jacob on Poetry." MLR, 69 (Apr., 1974), 290-296.
———. "Conversation With God: An Aspect of Dialogism in Jacob's Lyrical Poems." *Folio,* No. 9 (Oct., 1976), 33-37.
Simon, Pierre Henri. "Max Jacob: La Défense de Tartufe, Le Terrain Bouchaballe." *Le Monde,* 2-8 avr. 1964, p. 11.
Stein, Gertrude. "Eternité du poete." *Aguedal,* 4ᵉ ann., No. 2, "Hommage à Max Jacob" (mai, 1939), 168.
Szigeti, Robert. "Amitié de Max Jacob." *Europe,* Nos. 348-49 (avr.-mai, 1958), 32-37.
Thau, Annette. "Poetry and Antipoetry: A Study of Selected Aspects of Max Jacob's Poetic Style with an Introduction to his Esthetics." DA, 28 (1967), 1830A.
———. "The Esthetic Reflections of Max Jacob." FR, 45 (March, 1972), 800-812.

Thau, Annette. "Play with Words and Sounds in the Poetry of Max Jacob." RLM, Nos. 336-339 (1973), 125-156.

———. "Max Jacob's Letters to Gertrude Stein: A Critical Study." *Folio*, No. 9 (Oct. 1976), 47-54.

———. "Max Jacob and Cubism." RLM, Nos. 474-478 (1976), 145-72.

Thomas, Henri. "La Comédie Bouchaballe." RLM, Nos. 474-478 (1976), 19-22.

"Une conversion." *Almanach des lettres françaises et étrangères*, 1re ann. (janv.-fév.-mars, 1924), 358.

Valmy-Baysse, Jean. "Souvenir sur Max Jacob." *Aguedal*, 4e ann., No. 2 (mai, 1939), 169-173.

Villard, René. "A Max le jongleur de Notre-Dame." *Aguedal*, 4.e ann., No. 2, Hommage à Max Jacob" (mai, 1939), 187-189.

www.ingramcontent.com/pod-product-compliance
Lightning Source LLC
Chambersburg PA
CBHW020419230426
43663CB00007BA/1233